Calm

365 ways to a better you

Everyday
Calm

365 ways to a better you

Laurel Alexander

Illustrated by Michelle Tilly

spruce

An Hachette UK Company
First published in Great Britain in 2009 by Spruce
a division of Octopus Publishing Group Ltd
2–4 Heron Quays, London E14 4JP.
www.octopusbooks.co.uk
www.octopusbooksusa.com

Distributed in the US and Canada for Octopus Books USA
c/- Hachette Book Group USA
237 Park Avenue
New York NY 10017.

Produced by **Bookworx**
Editorial Jo Godfrey Wood, **Design** Peggy Sadler

ISBN 13 978-1-84601-316-4
ISBN 10 1-84601-316-X

A CIP catalogue record for this book is available from the British Library.

Printed and bound in China

10 9 8 7 6 5 4 3 2 1

Contents

Introduction

Wouldn't it be great if you could feel calm all of the time? Sounds like a great idea doesn't it? Well, this practical little book sets out 365 days' worth of easy activities that you can do for yourself to help you achieve serenity in your daily life.

'Stress' is a much-bandied-about word these days. There is 'good' stress; the kind of stress that gives you some get up and go when you need to get an important task done. And then there's the 'bad' stress that will achieve little and simply winds you up. Chronic stress, if you are unlucky enough to suffer from it, can lead to physical illness, psychological impairment and may adversely affect your everyday life.

So it's a very good idea to try to manage and reduce your stress levels. This book doesn't guarantee you won't ever feel stressed again, but it does set out a number of highly accessible and practical ideas that will help you to calm down and to enjoy life more fully.

Each day, you can read about an idea, that will inspire you to implement a chill-pill. These ideas are wide-ranging. You can discover how you can use nutrition, herbs, meditation, exercise, practical

activities, crystals, supplements, philosophical concepts, lifestyle changes and yoga to influence how calm you feel. Peppered throughout the book are 'instant calm' notes for those moments when you need to feel calm – NOW! Then every so often, scattered amongst the pearls of calm, you'll find quotes to get you thinking and inspire you toward serenity.

Calm is an achievable state of mind and stress is your response to an event. The same event could happen to you or to me, but it is our individual mind-sets that determine how we respond. This book will help you to discover a range of techniques to enable you to remain calm in the face of adversity and move yourself toward a healthier and more relaxed you.

By making small daily changes, you can change the stress habits of a lifetime and release the calm goddess within.

How to use this book

If you've bought this book as part of your plan for the New Year, that's fine, but if you've picked it up at some time during the middle of the year, don't worry. It will still work for you. You don't have to start it on New Year's Day; you can start any time you feel like it during the year. Just turn to Day 1 and work your way through the days in order. You will find that the months have either 30 or 31 days to reflect the real year, so you might want to match the month you're in with one that has the correct number of days on offer (the first month has 31 days).

At the end of every month you'll find a page for assessing how you're getting on. This is just an opportunity to think about what you've read and whether any of the ideas are working for you. There's also a space here to write down your thoughts and think about how you're getting on. Run out of writing space? Turn to the final pages of the book and you'll find more pages to continue any important personal notes.

day 1 Take a mind holiday

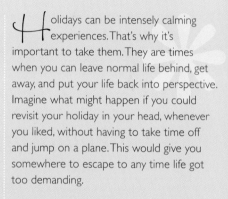

Instant calm

VISUALIZATION
Close your eyes, take a deep breath and relax your whole body. In your mind's eye visit your favorite place. After approximately ten minutes, open your eyes and slowly come back to reality. See how calm you feel.

Holidays can be intensely calming experiences. That's why it's important to take them. They are times when you can leave normal life behind, get away, and put your life back into perspective. Imagine what might happen if you could revisit your holiday in your head, whenever you liked, without having to take time off and jump on a plane. This would give you somewhere to escape to any time life got too demanding.

Remember a place where you went on holiday. Perhaps it's a special place in nature that makes you feel peaceful. Hold that image in your mind's eye. Rest with this image, allowing yourself to enjoy its tranquility. Practice this mind holiday regularly. Now you'll always have a special sanctuary to escape to whenever you need to regain your calm.

Since brain chemical serotonin levels enable you to maintain good sleep patterns and sleep quality, your appetite and your mood in general, reduction of serotonin causes you to feel less calm than usual. So, in times of anxiety and stress, your body needs to produce more of it.

You can do this by increasing the amounts of foods you eat that contain the amino acid L-tryptophan, so boosting serotonin levels, easing anxiety and bringing about calm.

These foods include: chocolate (yes!), oats, bananas, dried dates, milk, yogurt, cottage cheese, meat, fish, turkey, chicken, sesame seeds, chickpeas and peanuts. If you can't eat enough of these foods to make a difference, try taking the supplement 5-HTP.

Make a dream sachet

It can be very comforting and effective to sleep with a herb sachet tucked into your pillowcase. The herbs in the following blend are traditionally associated with good-quality rest and good dreams. Combine them with calming oils and create a dream-inspiring sachet to slip into your pillow at night. Mix together one-quarter of a cup each of hop flowers, dried rose petals and lavender flowers. Add five drops each of chamomile essential oil and lavender essential oil.

Fill a cotton drawstring bag or handkerchief with the mixture and tie it up securely with a pretty ribbon.

This simple yoga pose will help you to let go of whatever agitating thoughts you have been experiencing through the day and bring about a sense of deep calm.

Lie on your back with your eyes closed. Let your entire body relax and sink into the floor. Focus on your breath. Inhale through your nose, noticing how your abdomen rises. Breathe out through your mouth and notice how your abdomen sinks. Repeat the words 'calm mind' to yourself. If you get distracted, bring your attention back to your breathing. Thoughts may pop up, but don't get distracted by them. The spaces between them will get longer and your sense of calm will increase.

The more tranquil a man becomes, the greater is his success, his influence, his power for good. Calmness of mind is one of the beautiful jewels of wisdom.

James Allen

Go swimming today

It's hard to beat swimming when it comes to a sport or activity that strengthens your body and calms your mind. It relieves your mind from stress and tension, regulates your breathing, stimulates your circulation, while putting negligible stress on your joints.

So go and swim a lap or two today, just for fun. Feeling your body being supported effortlessly in water is comforting, while the repetitive action of swimming is soothing and meditative.

Carbohydrates are great for their calming effect on your brain chemistry. So if you eat foods that are high in vitamin B$_6$ and carbohydrates, you should notice the difference pretty quickly.

The most easily available carbs to try are: raisins (you could have them covered in chocolate, of course: even better!), whole-grain cereals, bananas and potatoes.

Breakfast is an important meal; it sets you up for the day ahead and this is the perfect opportunity to pack in some calming carbs.

Instant calm

BREAKFAST SUGGESTION

Try a bowl of oats or granola topped with a tempting sprinkling of raisins and chopped banana. Add a large spoonful of plain yogurt. No need for sugar; your breakfast is already sweet enough.

Instant calm

MEDITATION
Lie or sit quietly with your eyes closed. Breathe steadily in and out. Turn your attention to each part of your body in turn. First your forehead, then your chin, shoulders, neck and so on. Tell each part to relax and be calm.

How often do you find yourself being wound up by other people and losing your sense of calm? You might be having a bad-hair day or suffering from PMS, but sometimes you'll feel stressed for no particular reason. You may suddenly find yourself ready to do battle with someone over the slightest thing and this can be destructive, not to mention dangerous.

It's at these times that you need to take a deep breath, step back and ask yourself why you are so wound up. It might be that the person you want to attack reminds you of a hyper-critical aunt. Or perhaps this person is displaying an emotion that you are denying in yourself. Often you can let go of an unfounded irritation when you look within and are honest with yourself. Then you can begin to regain balance and peace.

When you feel upset, it's all too easy to lose perspective on your life temporarily. You tend to see the negative aspects of every situation and sometimes it seems impossible to see the positive parts.

To help you to regain perspective and calm down, imagine that you're looking at yourself from the other side of the room. In a detached way, observe how you are behaving and the thoughts that are passing through your mind. Imagine that you are your own best friend. What advice can you give to yourself to help you calm down, so that you can handle the situation better?

Instant calm

CALMING COMMUTE

If you find commuting to work stressful, put your amethyst in your pocket, so that you can hold it when you feel your stress levels rising. You'll be surprised how calming this simple act can be.

Crystals and semi-precious stones can have a stabilizing effect on your well-being and they can be a good focus for meditation. The amethyst, a beautiful mauve or purple stone, is one of the most effective crystals to use if you are feeling upset. Its calming attributes can relax the mind. It has a gently sedative energy that promotes peacefulness, happiness and contentment.

If you'd like to meditate with this stone, lie on your back and place it on your forehead, on your 'third eye' (the point between your eyebrows). Close your eyes. Take a deep breath and exhale completely. Do this six times. With each in-breath, say to yourself the word 'calm' and with each out-breath, say to yourself the word 'relax'.

Simple, ordinary, walking lowers stress and promotes a feeling of calmness. It reduces tiredness and gives you more energy for everyday tasks. If you have problems sleeping, walking can promote better-quality sleep. A 30-minute walk will work wonders, so instead of your regular bus ride, try walking to work or back home afterwards. If your journey is too long to walk the whole way, try just walking for part of it. Or have a brisk walk at lunchtime or instead of your usual coffee break.

Don't just walk 'there and back'; look around you at the people, the environment and at nature. Take your time and breathe in the (hopefully) fresh air. Be mindful of where you are, what you are doing and allow yourself to feel calmer with each step you take.

Homeopathy is a medicine that treats 'like' with 'like', using highly diluted solutions of remedies to promote healing. *Nux vomica* is a homeopathic remedy that is suitable if you are a workaholic, competitive, ambitious type of person; anything but calm, in fact. You might tend to be over-critical of yourself and others.

If you are impatient and tend to over-indulge in food, drink and coffee, you might find that nux vomica can calm you down. Take 30c before you go to sleep and you'll find that you feel that bit more sprightly in the morning.

eeling a bit agitated? The color blue may be able to help you. If you already have some blue items of clothing in your wardrobe, choose something blue to wear today. Or you could set the background color of your computer screen to an azure blue, just for the day.

Blue is the color of calmness, repose and unity. Looking at blue relaxes your central nervous system by producing chemicals that reduce your blood pressure, pulse and respiration rate. When you are unwell, the physiological need for blue actually increases! The associations with blue are those of tranquility, contentment and of being at peace.

Instant calm

CALMING LAPIS
Try placing a piece of deep blue lapis lazuli on your desk to look at in odd moments. You'll find it has a calming effect. Alternatively, wear some blue or turquoise beads. Blue lace agate, sodalite, turquoise, blue topaz and aventurine are other possible choices.

A 'peace' of chocolate

A CALMING CUP

Make yourself a big mug of hot chocolate, put your feet up and wait for calm to sink in.

Everyone seems to love chocolate and there's a good reason for this. So eating a little every now and again may not be as harmful as you suppose. Chocolate is packed with mood-enhancing chemicals; it's full of sugar, which is a carbohydrate, and it triggers the release of serotonin (a feel-good chemical) in the brain. It also contains fat, which satisfies your urge to take calories into your body.

Chocolate contains the same mood-enhancing chemical that is found in marijuana, although in much smaller quantities, and it also contains caffeine, although less than that found in coffee. The best chocolate to have, to benefit from these calming effects, is dark chocolate.

How often do you use the word 'should' in your daily life? Have you ever noticed how this word adds to the pressure that you put on yourself? Maybe your inner voice is continually telling you that you 'should' have done this or you 'should' do that.

'Should' implies you could do better or that you might be doing something wrong. Now think of the word 'could'. This word gives you a choice: it softens the impact of what you need to do. If you eradicate the word 'should' and substitute 'could', you might feel better and not so stressed. Just for today, try substituting 'should' for 'could' and see how much more in control and calm you feel.

Try a little acupressure

Acupressure is an ancient technique that uses finger pressure on specific points of the body to stimulate the vital flow of energy. It can be used to ease anxiety and help you experience calm.

Try this simple acupressure exercise. Clench your fist to make the tendons show. To find the acupressure point between the two main tendons along your inner forearm, measure two thumb-widths down from the skin crease across your wrist. Relax your hand while pressing this point with your thumb, until you feel a 'comfortable' pain. Hold the pressure while you knead the point with very small circular movements, for about a minute. Repeat the same action on the other arm.

See a friend

This is the day for you to do breakfast, lunch, tea or dinner with a friend. Friends benefit one another in lots of different ways. They listen, they encourage each other, they give advice, have fun, exchange trivia, share confidences and are simply there for one another. They can even help out with practical problems, if that's what's needed. The health benefits of friendship are wide-ranging, including living a longer, healthier life. On top of this, being a good friend makes your life more fun, interesting, and easier to handle.

Another health benefit of friendship is that when you have even one best, or close, friend, your ability to deal with stress and problems is greatly increased.

Make lavender-honey

SWEET DREAMS!
For sleep help, sprinkle two drops of lavender essential oil on your pillow at night.

Lavender has a soothing, sedative effect and is well known for balancing mind and body. If you love a dollop of honey on your toast in the mornings, why not try adding lavender to it, to get the added value of its calming properties?

Take 226 g (8 oz) of clover honey and four tablespoons of the dried lavender buds. Heat the honey through in a double-boiler. Add the lavender and stir. Continue to stir over the heat for 30 minutes. Remove it from the heat and allow to cool slightly. Strain out the lavender and put the honey in a jar.

Whether you write your own poetry or just love other people's, fill up your journal pages with poetry that has a calming effect on you. If you don't feel inspired to write your own, don't worry, just write down your thoughts in a poetic way. Search for words that are evocative and appealing to you.

Hunt down books you love, or use the Internet or magazines to find words of wisdom. Whenever you come across a special gem that resonates with you, copy it, cut it out, or print it out and stick it into your journal to read at those times when you need calming, encouraging words.

Instant calm

YOUR JOURNAL
Decorating your own journal is a satisfying, calming thing to do. Just take an ordinary plain notebook and fill it with your own writing, day by day. No need to plan; just write whatever comes into your head. Now take bright felt-tip pens and doodle around the margins of the pages.

Sip sweet potato soup

Some recipes are wonderfully calming, as well as absolutely delicious. The low-GI wonder-food (see page 45), sweet potato, has a soothing effect, while a little bit of spice lifts your mood. And it's really easy to make into this delicious soup, too.

Melt 40 g (1 oz) butter in a pan and soften half an onion and crushed clove of garlic over a gentle heat. Dry-fry four teaspoonfuls of cumin seeds in another pan for two minutes. Then add it to the softened onion along with half a peeled and sliced yam, water and chicken-stock cube. Simmer for ten minutes, or until the potato softens. Then blend in a food-processor. Serve with a spoonful of delicious, creamy fromage frais.

Make an aroma blend

After a high-stress activity, such as meeting a tight deadline, try this simple way of burning calming essential oils and creating a relaxing atmosphere at home.

Light a large pillar candle. Wait for a few moments for the wax on the top of the candle to melt, and then blow the candle out. Add a calming blend of two drops of juniper, two drops of cedarwood and two drops of bergamot to the melted wax before relighting the candle.

Put on some soothing music, kick off your shoes, dim the lights, put your feet up and enjoy that glass of wine!

Instant calm

A SINGLE CANDLE
Try lighting one candle. It will have an automatic calming effect on everyone in the room.

Conjure up a calm image

Visualization, whereby you imagine something so strongly that it seems 'real' to you and to your body, is a powerful way of influencing your mood.

Try this calming visualization. Imagine something that suggests 'calm' to you, but imagine it huge. You could visualize a vast spreading oak tree, a still pool of water, the palm of Buddha or Christ, a giant mother's lap, or a big cloud of pink light; whatever pops into your head. Fill up your whole mind with this image.

We are not human beings having a spiritual experience. We are spiritual beings having a human experience.

Pierre Teilhard de Chardin

If you are experiencing stress, a sure way to release it is to get your body moving. One quick and easy way is to put on some loud music and just dance. This can be any style you like, but the more energetic it is, the more effective it will be.

Moving to music stimulates your senses and is great for both body and mind. All in all, this will make you a calmer, fitter, sexier and a much more confident person!

Instant calm

JOGGING
If you're not into dancing, you may find jogging more your kind of thing, and this will have the same calming effect as dancing. Just put on your comfortable jogging gear, grab your bottle of water and go!

Make a pot pourri

FOCUSING

Sit in front of your pot pourri for ten minutes. Gaze at it, eyes half-closed, or close your eyes. Focus on your breath, watch it come in and then leave you again. Open your eyes. You'll feel calm pervade your whole body.

Pot pourris are wonderful things to have in your home. You can dot them around in different places, using beautiful bowls and containers to add to their appeal. They make great focal points.

For a truly calming aroma that will be suitable for any room, mix together four cups of dried lavender blossoms, two cups of dried rose geranium leaves, two cups of dried rosemary, 30 g (1 oz) of orris root and between three and six drops of lavender oil. Blend the herbs and oil with the orris root and place the mixture in a tightly sealed container. Let it ferment for four to six weeks, shaking daily. When the aroma starts to fade, just add a few drops of lavender, rosemary and rose geranium to the blend and mix together. Place it in a pretty bowl.

appy relationships with close family members, friends or others are important for your peace of mind. Accepting help and support from those who care about you and will listen to you strengthens your resilience in times of crisis.

You might find that being active in community groups, faith-based organizations or other local groups provides social support and can help you if you need to reclaim hope, for some reason. This way, you can also help others.

Assisting others in their times of need can also benefit you in making connections. Consider your social networks. How do you make connections? With whom? How do these networks benefit you?

Instant calm

JUST SMILE
Today, decide to smile at everyone you meet, whether you know them or not.

Perfume your life with calming fragrances. Take a fragrance ring (a ceramic disk that you can impregnate with a few drops of essential oil) and place it on top of an ordinary light bulb (for example, use the lamp on your bedside table). The warmth from the bulb releases the aromatic vapor into the atmosphere.

Another idea is to place a few drops of the essential oil directly onto a cold light bulb/desk lamp and then switch on the light.

Choose from a combination of the following chill-out oils: lavender, Roman chamomile, ylang ylang, sandalwood, frankincense, rosewood or clary sage.

Take a half-day off

Book a half-day off and do squiddly-diddly. Go out for tea or coffee. Wander round town or go for a country walk. Or spend a half-day day in bed. Avoid using your phone or computer; eat or sleep when you want. Let the sheer joy of taking time out bring you a sense of calm.

Worry on Friday

If you find yourself being something of a worry-bucket, try saving all your worries up for Friday afternoon. By the time it comes along, you will probably have forgotten what half of your worries were about and the other half will have sorted out, all by themselves.

Eat to sleep

CALMING SNACK
For a good-night snack try low-fat biscuits, a glass of milk, popcorn or fresh fruit and yogurt.

If you get good-quality sleep you'll find it's a whole lot easier to keep calm during your daily life. There is a crucial link between what you eat and the quality of your sleep, so avoid eating heavy meals late at night, as this will activate your digestion and keep you awake.

Spicy and gas-forming foods can also contribute to poor sleep quality and even insomnia. A glass or two of your favorite alcoholic drink is fine up to a point, but if you drink too much alcohol, it will act as a stimulant that will keep you awake as well. However, did you know that low blood sugar, through lack of food, can also cause insomnia? The best option is to eat your evening meal early, followed by a light snack before bed, if you're feeling peckish.

Derived from two Sanskrit words 'ha' (Sun, or the breath of the Sun) and 'tha' (Moon, or the breath of the moon), hatha yoga is the most popular form of yoga and the basis for a number of other different forms. A typical hatha yoga position is the Front Corpse Pose, which you will find has noticeably calming effects.

Lie down on your front, legs slightly apart, toes touching, and allow your heels to fall out to the sides. Make a pillow with your hands. Lengthen your body, tense and relax the muscles. Feel your body sinking into the floor as you exhale.

Cosmic laughter

Instant calm

LAUGHING BUDDHA

Try this meditation to help you laugh for no reason at all. When you wake up, stretch your whole body and start to laugh. Just lift the corners of your mouth and laugh. Forced laughter will stimulate the real thing and affect your mood for the whole day. Do it for five to ten minutes.

Laughter is a highly effective way of releasing stress and calming down. Medically, it has been shown to lower blood pressure, reduce stress hormones and boost immune function. Laughter also triggers the release of endorphins, the body's natural painkillers, and produces a general sense of wellbeing.

Spontaneous mirth is something you can allow to happen naturally, through your natural sense of relaxation and fun. So today, make a point of looking for more of the funny, ridiculous and incongruous events that go on around you in your everyday life.

he aura is the body's energy field around your physical body. You can stroke it or smooth it, and so calm it down.

Try using a white feather to brush your aura; very similar to using a smudge stick (see page 49). You flick the feather all around your body in outward motions, to brush away the negativity. You can also use your fingers to brush negative energy away into the atmosphere.

Imagine that all the little bits of negativity are being swept into a container. When the container is full, imagine it going deep into outer space and being emptied, leaving you feeling calm and refreshed.

Instant calm

GROUNDING
Ordinary activities can calm and ground you. Try washing your hands and face with cold water.

checklist 1 *How did you do?*

Whether you tried out several ideas this month or just one, you might like to reflect on what you chose to try and why, and if it worked for you.

1. How many activities did you try this month?

- 1–3 activities ☐
- 4–10 activities ☐
- 11–20 activities ☐
- 20–31 activities ☐

2. How many did you repeat several times in the month?

- 1–3 activities ☐
- 4–10 activities ☐
- 11–20 activities ☐
- 20–31 activities ☐

3. Which activities had a positive effect on your mood this month?

Use the page opposite to make notes about what worked for you and what didn't.

Notes, jottings and thoughts

day

32 Thought-stopping

Instant calm

STOP SIGNS
When you are driving
and see a 'Stop' sign,
recall today's visualization.
Don't forget to stop the
car as well!

If a worry won't leave you alone, use a wonderful technique called 'thought-stopping'. Take a few minutes to sit down, close your eyes and say to yourself silently: 'stop' or 'go away'.

You might want to visualize a red traffic sign with the word 'stop' on it. In addition, if it helps, you could wear an elastic band around your wrist as a reminder. Just twang it whenever you want to stop a thought.

Meditating on space, the heavens and the stars takes you out of yourself temporarily, allowing you to focus on life outside and beyond yourself and your world, so that you lose yourself in a feeling of calmness. This helps you to put your worries into perspective.

Sit down, preferably in a still, dark and quiet area outdoors and observe the heavens. The vastness of space is awesome. You might find that you can make a lot of your problems seem very small and insignificant.

Instant calm

TIGER'S EYE
Wear a tiger's eye
stone to help you feel
grounded, optimistic,
balanced and calm.

The energy field around your physical body is called the 'subtle energy body', or aura, and extends beyond your physical body. It consists of levels of energy oscillating around your body, like an opalescent egg-shaped bubble. Within this bubble and connecting to your spinal area are energy centers called chakras.

The root chakra (related to the area at the base of your spine) corresponds to your need for stability and security. If you don't feel secure or stable, your ability to be calm will be affected, indicating that this chakra may be out of balance. You can help rebalance it through imagining yourself to be a tree, feeling secure and grounded, with roots going from your feet deep down into the Earth.

The Glycemic Index (GI) is a measure of the effects of carbs on your blood glucose levels and carb intake has a marked influence on your mood. Carbs that break down rapidly during digestion, releasing glucose quickly into your bloodstream, have a high GI (for example, chocolate). Those that break down slowly, releasing glucose gradually into your bloodstream, have a low GI and give you more energy, so have a calming effect on your system.

So today, begin to include more fruit and vegetables in your diet. In addition, include grainy breads, pasta, legumes and pulses, milk and foods low in carbohydrates such as fish, eggs, meat, nuts and oils.

The feel-good chemical, serotonin, cannot be produced by the body without L-tryptophan and without serotonin, you tend to feel low. Pineapple is a natural source of tryptophan, so it's worth trying to include it in your diet.

This simple recipe makes a delicious dessert or snack. Combine half a cup of yogurt, two tablespoons of honey and a little crystallized ginger. Cover and chill it thoroughly. To serve, spoon the sour cream mixture over a small tin of drained, chilled pineapple or chunks of fresh pineapple.

Try this simple walking meditation to calm a troubled mind. Start walking at a normal pace. Be aware of your foot as the heel first makes contact with the ground. It rolls forward onto the ball of your foot, lifts, then travels through the air again.

Think about the different sensations in your feet, ankles and lower legs. Be aware of the whole of your pelvis. One side of your hip moves forward and then the other; one hip lifts while the other sinks. Notice your shoulders and how they move in opposition to your hips. Be aware of the motions in your arms and hands and notice your neck and the muscles supporting your skull. Relax your jaw and let your eyes be softly focused. Lastly, come to a stop and just experience yourself calmly standing.

There is absolutely no reason for being rushed along with the rush. Everybody should be free to go slow.

Robert Frost

47

Enjoy Asian ginseng

CALMING DECOCTION

Place 15 g (½ oz) cinnamon bark, 1-cm (½-in) piece of ginseng root and 500 ml (1 pint) water in a pan. Bring to the boil and simmer, covered, for 20 minutes. Strain and drink twice daily.

Asian ginseng has a history of herbal use going back over 5,000 years. It can be used to increase your stamina and wellbeing and has long been valued for its ability to help the body deal with stress.

You can take ginseng root in a Korean soup-based dish called *Samgyetang* (sometimes called 'chicken ginseng soup'). It is basically a whole young chicken stuffed with glutinous rice and boiled in a broth of Korean ginseng, dried, seeded jujube fruits, garlic and ginger.

A word of warning: you need to consult with a professional herbalist before you take ginseng in any form.

Smudging is the burning of certain herbs such as sage, cedar or sweet grass, to create a cleansing smoke bath, which can then be used to purify both people and the space around them.

The burning of herbs is a ritual for cleansing, purifying and protecting your physical and spiritual bodies. The effect of the smoke is to banish negative energies, thereby leaving you feeling positive, balanced and calm.

You can buy ready-made sage smudge sticks, which you light, allowing the smoke to waft around your body or around the room.

Instant calm

FREE-FORM ART

Take a blank sheet of paper and a collection of colored felt-tip pens. Without thinking, just spontaneously start drawing, letting your hand move wherever it wants to go.

Using painting or drawing as a release from tension isn't about technique or talent. It's about doodling, using color, creating patterns and playing with shapes.

You could use charcoal, pencil, pen or paint and you might want to use craft items such as glitter, pipe-cleaner bits, felt, colored pens, stick-on stars and shapes. How about trying play dough or modeling clay?

The potential of art as a therapeutic tool became apparent after World War Two, when survivors of the war used art in hospitals and rehabilitation centers to help overcome the traumas they had experienced. You can play with art as a way of releasing and calming your mind.

Who are your friends?

List all the friends you feel closest to, including those who have been a source of warmth in your past. Identify those you would like to be closer to on another list. Now make a third list of what you would like to talk about, or do, with each friend. Is there anyone you would like to ring right now?

Choose rose quartz

Rose quartz, associated with love and self-healing, is a gentle, pale- to medium-pink quartz. It is a stone of gentle warmth and love, able to help heal emotional wounds and pain. Just having one near you, perhaps on your desk, will help to calm you and open your heart to peace.

For a soothing night's sleep, make yourself a dream pillow. Blend the following dried herbs in an airtight container and leave for seven days: half a cup each of mugwort, lavender, hops, rosemary and one cup of rose petals.

Next, fold a 12 × 30-cm (5 × 12-in) strip of fabric in half and sew both sides, leaving the top open. Turn the pillow inside out and place a small handful of a 'fiber-fill'-type product in the bottom. Then put a quarter cup of the mix on top, before adding another handful of 'fiber-fill' to the herbs. The extra filling makes the pillow more comfortable to sleep on. Sew up the opening and place your dream pillow inside a pillowcase to get a calming night's sleep.

Balance is a metaphor for life. If you are out of balance, your life will be too. But you can regain it if you are aware of your centre. Alexander Technique re-educates the body through physical and psychological principles. The following exercise helps you establish body balance:

1. Notice how you distribute your weight over your feet. Look at your shoe heels.
2. Using a mirror, look at your line of balance (an imaginary line passing from your crown, through your spinal column, through the pelvis, hip joint, knee joint and through your heel into the ground).
3. Stand on both feet and let yourself sway slowly backward and forward.
4. Make the swaying movements smaller and smaller until you notice you are in your optimum line of balance.

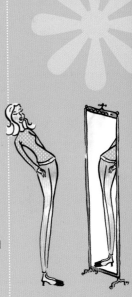

Qi Gung is an ancient Chinese discipline in which energy is harnessed to combat illness and promote longevity. Try this exercise to calm yourself:

Stand with your feet shoulder-width apart, knees slightly bent and tailbone tucked in. Lift your head and tuck your chin in. Look forward and let your shoulders relax, arms hanging, palms toward your thighs. Turn your palms face to the front and inhale. Arc your arms up to head-height, elbows slightly bent. Straighten your body. Now turn your arms so that your palms face the ground. Exhale. Arc your arms down to your thighs and sink down, bending from your waist with knees bent. Turn your arms so that your palms face out to the back. Repeat four times. Inhale, raise and straighten your body and turn your palms to face your thighs once again.

Sit or lie comfortably, relax your body, close your eyes and take some deep breaths. Mentally scan one particular muscle as you inhale. As you exhale, imagine the tension releasing as that muscle relaxes. After several breaths, move your awareness to another area.

Systematically scan your entire body: begin at your scalp and work down through your face, eyes, jaw, neck, shoulders, arms, hands, back, thighs, legs and feet. For each tight area, mentally repeat 'warmth and heaviness are flowing into my…'. If your mind wanders, just bring your attention back and continue scanning your body until you feel completely relaxed.

Be inspired by plants

Plants you can grow and nurture yourself are truly calming, and so wandering around a nursery or garden center can be a real chill-out experience. Whatever the time of year, there is always something to look at and feel inspired by.

Whether you want some indoor plants to adorn your home, small items to put in a window box or outdoor plants, such as small trees, to replenish your garden, you'll find something tempting that you can nurture and grow.

Bach Flower Remedies are flower essences, suspended in alcohol, designed to work on the emotions. The remedy called aspen is good to use if you have vague fears but you don't know where they come from. It may seem as though there is no explanation. You know this, yet you still feel terrified that something negative is going to happen.

These vague, unexplainable fears may haunt you night or day. A typical time when you might need aspen is when you wake up in fear from a bad dream, even if you have already forgotten the dream itself. You may be afraid to tell your trouble to others. Take this precious Bach Flower Remedy to help towards an inner peace, security and fearlessness.

To be assertive is to be calm. You can follow this list to get yourself back in control:

- Look at your rights, what you want, need and feel about the problem.
- Arrange a time and place to discuss the problem.
- Define the problem as specifically as possible.
- Describe your feelings to another person using 'I' messages.
- Express your request – be specific and firm.
- Reinforce – describe positive consequences or, sometimes, negative ones.

Create a mantra

A mantra is a repeated sound or phrase that has a transformative effect. Repeating any word produces an actual physical vibration in your body and this can have a physical effect on you. If you say the word 'calm' again and again, then you will actually begin to feel calm.

Another aspect of mantras is 'intent'. If the actual physical vibration is coupled with your mental intention to make something happen, the vibration then contains a mental component, which influences the result of saying it. Here are some guidelines to follow when you create your mantra for calm: word your mantra in the present, keep your mantra short and to the point, believe your mantra is already a reality and expect the positive reality of calmness to occur.

Instant calm

ACT 'AS IF'

Whenever you need to give yourself a confidence-boost about a forthcoming plan, think about 'acting as if.' This means behaving as though your wish is already becoming a reality.

The B-vitamins are eight water-soluble vitamins that play important roles in your cell metabolism. Together, they help to combat the symptoms and causes of stress and help to keep you calm.

All B-vitamins are dispersed throughout the body. Most of them must be replenished daily, since excess is excreted. To increase your vitamin B intake today and boost your nervous system, tuck into a jacket potato with tuna or a lentil and turkey soup with chili peppers.

Consider how much information you absorb in just one day. You listen to the radio, watch the TV, speak on the phone, surf the Internet, see your friends, talk with people at work, rush to the shops, respond to emails and drive through town.

Just for today switch off your mobile, your computer and TV. Lessen the information overload that normally assails you and freewheel through your day with no technology and as little information as possible. You'll find that the overall effect is very calming.

Instant calm

LESS IS MORE
Whenever the complexity of your life is becoming overwhelming, think 'less is more'.

Alternate nose-breathing

To calm down or to ease a headache try this yogic breathing exercise. Close your right nostril with your right thumb and inhale through your left nostril. Do this to the count of four seconds. Close your left nostril with your right ring finger and little finger, and at the same time remove your thumb from your right nostril, and exhale through it. Do this to the count of eight. This completes a half-round.

Inhale through your right nostril to the count of four seconds. Close your right nostril with your right thumb and exhale through your left nostril to the count of eight. This completes one full round.

Start by doing three rounds, adding one per week until you are doing seven rounds.

Fiction is a great way to take a quick and immediate break, to be instantly transported into another world. There is something about stopping to focus on words arranged for your reading pleasure that is instantly relaxing. Reading takes your mind off your problems, has a therapeutic effect and is a timely circuit-breaker.

The expression 'curling up with a book' evokes a warm and cosy image and feels luxurious if you don't get to do it often. Reading is an easy and quick way to nourish your soul, because it is usually a solitary pursuit. Curl up now and try it out.

Run a warm bath and add a blend of essential oils to your bath milk or bath oil: 24 drops of neroli, 12 drops of clary sage, 12 drops of lavender and six drops of cedarwood. Light some candles, put on soft music and slip into your relaxing bath.

Before getting down to the soaping and cleansing bit, lie back with your eyes closed. Take a few deep breaths and allow the tension to flow out of you into the water and disperse. Imagine with every in-breath that you are breathing in relaxation and peace of mind.

How do you react to change? Do you resist it because it feels like a threat? When you initiate change, you feel in control. But if the change happens to you (for example, if you are made redundant from a job), you may well feel upset and out of control; far from calm.

It's at times of enforced change that it's good to try to alter your perspective and see change as opportunity for unexpected, positive outcomes. At such times, familiar habits may help to keep you stable; these are under your control. These include activities such as walking the dog. Stability and familiarity create calmness during change. Think about a change taking place in your life now, or one that is about to happen. What can you do something about and what is outside your control?

A pedicure pep-up

Pampering, such as giving yourself a pedicure, can bring calm during stormy times.

1. First add your favorite essential oil to warm water and soak your feet for ten minutes.
2. Dry your feet and exfoliate them, especially your heels. Remove dry skin with a mixture of olive oil and salt or sugar, and rinse.
3. Cut your nails with a clipper and file them to your length of choice.
4. Massage your feet with a rich cream. Apply cuticle oil to your nails to soften and revitalize any rough areas.
5. Use a cuticle stick to press the cuticles back neatly.
6. Apply a base coat of polish. Then apply two further thin coats. Finish with a final top coat.

Try sandalwood

Sandalwood oil calms the mind and has a harmonizing effect. It is perfect if you have a hectic lifestyle and are prone to feeling stressed. Try blending it with ylang ylang (good for easing tension), and putting it in a burner. The fragrance will permeate your home and help you to feel calm.

Feel-good citrine

The gemstone citrine is pale yellowish-green color. It is like a good friend who encourages you and gives you self-confidence. Its emotional qualities are optimism, hope and warmth. Wear citrine to help banish negativity and inspire enthusiasm, all adding up to a calmer you.

Calming embroidery

Many craft activities are repetitive and therefore very calming. Have you ever tried embroidery? This is a really soothing activity, a lot easier to master than you might think and it can be a great way to customize clothes. For example, you can give an old pair of jeans a new lease of life by embroidering colorful flowers on them.

Besides normal embroidery thread, you can also embroider with other materials such as metal thread, tiny beads, feathers and sequins. You can also machine-embroider using a sewing machine. Search the Internet for sites aimed at beginners or look around a bookshop to inspire you. Your nimble fingers will soon want to get going on this highly worthwhile and calming activity.

A head massage will relax and calm you, even if it's DIY. Massage a little almond oil into your head, starting from the sides, working toward the top, then toward the front, and finally to the back.

Grasp fistfuls of hair at the roots and tug gently, keeping the knuckles close to your scalp. Place the thumb of your left hand under the left occipital area (base of the head) and the thumb of your right hand under the right occipital area and relax the tight muscles by using a rubbing movement. Place your left hand on your right shoulder near your neck. Using medium pressure, squeeze the shoulder muscle that starts at the base of your neck. Work your way outward along your shoulder to your arm. Change arms and work the other side.

checklist 2 *How did you do?*

$\mathcal{W}$hether you tried out several ideas this month or just one, you might like to reflect on what you chose to try and why, and if it worked for you.

1. How many activities did you try this month?

- 1–3 activities ☐
- 4–10 activities ☐
- 11–20 activities ☐
- 20–30 activities ☐

2. How many did you repeat several times in the month?

- 1–3 activities ☐
- 4–10 activities ☐
- 11–20 activities ☐
- 20–30 activities ☐

3. Which activities had a positive effect on your mood this month?

Use the page opposite to make notes about what worked for you and what didn't.

Notes, jottings and thoughts

Aquamarine for serenity

Instant calm

WHILE YOU'RE MEDITATING

Hold or wear an aquamarine while you are meditating.

The beautifully colored aquamarine gemstone ranges in shade from blue to blue-green. Long known for helping us to see the good side of situations and attracting positive responses, its energies are calming and relaxing. You could use the stone to reduce stress and quieten your mind, thus clarifying perception, sharpening the intellect and removing any confusion.

Place a piece of aquamarine somewhere in your home or carry a small piece in your pocket. Every time you touch it or see it you can be reminded of its calming influences.

D° you often jump to conclusions, particularly assuming the worst outcome of any situation, thereby causing yourself more stress then necessary?

Perhaps you tend to focus on one aspect of a situation when forming a judgment. For example, maybe you assume you haven't received a phone call from a friend because she didn't like what you said to her. In reality, your friend probably didn't phone because she forgot, or something had distracted her, or maybe she was too busy. Jumping to conclusions is a pointless activity; it's a waste of time and it makes us tense.

Instant calm

DO SOME COUNTING!
See how many times today you can avoid jumping to conclusions and how much calmer you feel as a result.

Every time you drink tea, coffee or hot chocolate you're giving your body a hit of caffeine; perhaps not such a good idea if you're trying to reduce your stress levels. If you have more than two or three caffeine drinks per day your 'habit' may be affecting you emotionally and physically. As little as 20 mg of caffeine can produce noticeable body and mood changes.

Think about how much caffeine you are taking daily: an average cup of tea contains around 50 mg of caffeine, while an average cup of instant coffee contains around 70–100 mg. A 350-ml (12-oz) can of cola contains around 40 mg of caffeine and 28 g (10 oz) of chocolate contains about 10–15 mg. So if you are feeling in any way hyper, think before you drink or eat anything containing caffeine.

Being grounded is an important aspect of feeling calm. It really means that you are connected with the Earth and that you are centered.

Whenever you feel wobbly or 'spacey', try this. Sit or stand with your eyes closed and observe your breathing for a few minutes.

Visualize yourself as a tree, with your roots growing down into the Earth, through the soles of your feet. The energy of your being roots deep into the Earth and any excess is grounded within your strong roots. When you feel sufficiently anchored or earthed, bring yourself back into present reality.

Instant calm

GROUNDING BEFORE MEDITATION

If you are sitting in a chair to meditate, ground yourself by placing both feet flat on the floor first.

Try some iyengar yoga

All yoga has calming effects, but iyengar yoga can be extremely calming. It is known for its use of props, such as belts and blocks, to help you perform the postures comfortably.

Try the Restrained Angle Pose. Sit with legs stretched in front. Bend both legs and bring the feet toward your groin. Bring soles and heels together, holding the feet near the toes and bringing the heels near your perineum. The outer sides of the feet rest on the floor. Breathe normally. Widen your thighs and lower your knees to the floor.

Pull your heels closer to the perineum. Grip your feet firmly, press your knees, the ankles and the thighs to the floor and stretch your spine upward. Gaze ahead. Hold the pose for a minute, then release your feet, straighten your legs and relax.

$\mathcal{W}$hat you value is what you care about the most. Conditioning, education, the influences of parents, culture, are all sources of 'learned values', which become your subconscious values.

When you don't align your actions with your consciously chosen values, it means you're aligning your actions with someone else's. And this is the worst possible formula for achieving calmness.

When you consciously choose your values, YOU feel in control, rather than 'the system', or the authority figures or past influences in your life.

Today's thought

LIFE GOALS
Think about your life goals and consider whether they are yours or someone else's.

day 68

Try Southern Cross

Do you have a 'poor me' mentality? To relax into a positive attitude, take Southern Cross Australian Bush Essence to help you understand that you can change your situation by changing your thoughts. For example 'I'm always stressed', becomes 'I can change my mindset and relax more.'

day 69

Biochemic tissue salts

In the 19th century Dr Schussler identified 12 minerals that he believed to be vital to human health. These biochemic tissue salts are available as homeopathic formulations, which you can take as tablets dissolved under the tongue to help specifically in bringing about a natural calm. You can take them at any time.

Do some neck rotating

We tend to hold a lot of tension in the neck and shoulders. So it's a good idea to try and release it from time to time. If you feel that your neck is tense, try this quick relaxing exercise:

Sit upright in a firm chair. Relax and breathe deeply. Let your chin drop toward your chest. Continue to breathe while you slowly roll your head to the right, so that your right ear moves toward your shoulder. Slowly return to the original position with your chin dropped toward your chest. Complete five rotations to the right and five to the left. Afterwards you should feel much calmer.

YOUR GLASS OF WATER

Keep a full glass of water by you while you work and be sure to keep sipping from it throughout your working day. Try adding some drops of calming vervain, too!

If you tend to be highly strung and intense, perhaps using more force than necessary when you are performing practical tasks, the Bach Flower Remedy vervain may suit you.

You may be prone to strain and tension from pushing too hard, physically ending up with aches, pains and insomnia. A few drops in your glass of drinking water will help you to pull back, from time to time, so that your body and mind can be restored to calmness.

Try to prioritize

Having an endless and unachievable list of things on your 'to do' list can make you feel tense unless you prioritize them. Use this simple exercise to identify what order your tasks should be done in. Make a list containing at least ten items. Work through the following plan:

Place A against jobs you consider to be really important, Place B against jobs you consider not quite so important and place C against jobs you believe are unimportant. Go back through the list and eliminate all the Bs by reconsidering them as really important A or unimportant C. Now prioritize your As in terms of importance. Identify the most important and number it A1, then work through the list until you have numbered each one. Now concentrate your energy on carrying out the tasks on the A list.

Instant calm

WRITING THINGS DOWN

It will help to keep you calmer if you get into the habit of writing things down. This could be in the form of keeping lists and writing a regular journal. That way you don't have to keep everything in your head all at once; a sure recipe for tension and stress.

81

Instant calm

JASMINE IN YOUR BATH

After you have run your bath, shake several drops of jasmine oil into the water. Alternatively use it in your aromatherapy burner.

The name 'jasmine' is derived from the Persian word 'yasmin'. The Chinese, Arabs and Indians used the plant medicinally, as well as for aphrodisiac and ceremonial purposes.

Jasmine is a valuable remedy to soothe your nerves and produce a feeling of confidence, optimism and euphoria, while revitalizing and restoring energy.

A word of warning: it is advisable not to use jasmine if you're pregnant.

Do a Spinal Roll

If you're feeling particularly tense today, try this quickie to calm yourself down. Lie on your back and extend your arms out in a horizontal line from your shoulders, with your palms down.

Relax, breathe deeply and pull your knees up to your chest. Now roll your head to the right while rolling your hips to the left, until your legs are resting together on the floor. Rest, breathe and turn your head to the left while rolling your legs to the right, until they rest together on the floor.
Repeat this four times. Rest.

day 75 — One-breath relaxation

Instant calm

PEACE
When you are meditating, you might like to repeat to yourself silently the word 'peace' on the inhalation and 'calm' on the exhalation.

This is a relaxation technique that you can do anywhere, whenever you feel the need. Straighten your back, relax your shoulders and take in a slow, deep breath through your nose. Be aware of the breath coming into your body. How does it feel? Warm or cool? Hold your breath and as you exhale slowly through your mouth, release every bit of negativity and tension from your thoughts and body.

As you inhale deeply again, imagine yourself drawing the breath into every fiber of your being, every cell and every organ. Imagine a white light filling every corner of your mind.

Let go

Find a quiet place, lie or sit down, close your eyes and take in a deep breath. Give yourself full permission to let go of control. Repeat to yourself silently several times the words 'letting go'. Each time you exhale, imagine you're breathing all the tension out of your body. Repeat 'letting go' to yourself several times.

As your body relaxes and your emotions calm down, thoughts may slide through your mind. Don't resist these thoughts, since that will only make them more powerful.

Instant calm

FRESH AIR IN YOUR MEDITATION

Imagine that with each inhalation, fresh air is cleansing your mind of all the thoughts you don't need, leaving you feeling so much calmer than before.

'Liming' away the day

Liming is the Caribbean art of disengaging from the drive toward constant busyness and doing absolutely nothing instead.

Instead of being permanently 'busy' you can tell jokes, hum a song, read something light and inconsequential, sit in the garden, take a nap, look out of the window, daydream or meditate. Break away from the stress of clock-watching. Liming helps you move from human 'doing' to human 'being'.

Do a forward bend

If you're experiencing body tension, try this. Stand up straight, breathe deeply and raise your hands above your head.

Continue breathing deeply while you slowly bend forward, until your hands are dangling toward the floor. Don't bounce or strain. You might want to bend your knees slightly. Let your attention go to the stretch in your legs and lower back. Relax and breathe. Slowly return to the upright position.

Instant calm

GET UP FROM YOUR DESK

If you work at a desk, be sure to get up from it at frequent intervals and move around. This will help you regain perspective and calm in your working day.

day 79 *Eat chocky rice pud*

Instant calm

OVER THE TOP
For a totally over-the-top gesture, sprinkle crumbled chocolate over your pudding just before eating!

This is the ultimate comfort food. Indulge in this yummy chocolate pudding to release your mood-boosting endorphins to experience that calm feeling.

Preheat the oven to 150°C (300°F). Dissolve three tablespoonfuls of cocoa in four tablespoons of boiling water. Pour in one litre (four cups) of milk, stirring all the time. Add one tablespoon of vanilla extract and pour into a buttered dish. Add 100 g (3 oz) arborio rice and 100 g (3 oz) demerara sugar, stir, then cook in the oven for two hours.

Use an ionizer

*N*egative ions can increase your capacity to absorb and utilize oxygen, thereby improving overall health, endurance and calm. Ions are found everywhere in the air you breathe, but it is the proper balance between negative and positive ions that's important.

An air ionizer, apart from cleaning the air (this is good if you suffer from airborne allergies), has been reported to be helpful if you suffer from Seasonal Affective Disorder (SAD). Ionizers can also help relieve tension and improve sleep. Buy a negative ionizer today for your home or car and increase your sense of calm.

Surrender expectations

'SURRENDER'
Think about this word and all it means. Look it up in a dictionary and contemplate it deeply. If you assumed it had a negative spin, think again. There may be more in the word than you had thought.

When you have expectations, you have preconceived ideas of how things should be. You expect things to happen in a certain way and this prevents you from seeing how things really are. This stops you recognizing the good when it comes your way.

Without preconceived ideas to limit your perception, you are able to accept what comes your way as part of the solution.

You can always experience more when you are in a place of no expectations than from a place of having fixed expectations. So try surrendering to your expectations today and observe how good things come to you when you least expect them.

Letting go

To visualize 'floating' is a letting go of everything; a very important aspect of keeping calm.

Try this calming visualization. Lie down and let go of your muscles, your body, your bones, your thoughts and your feelings. Just let yourself sink into the bed or the floor and don't do anything at all.

Every time you become aware of a thought or an emotion, let it go from your mind and breathe it out of your system. This causes you to become totally limp, without boundaries, gently awake and gently aware. You're floating out of a feeling of tension and into calmness.

A SINGLE GREEN LEAF

The next time you are outdoors, pick a green leaf, put it in a small vase and place it where you can see it during your day. It will help to calm and ground you in odd moments.

On physical and emotional levels, the color green helps your heart to bring you physical equilibrium and relaxation. Green relaxes your muscles and helps you breathe more deeply and slowly.

It creates feelings of comfort, laziness, relaxation and calm and helps you to balance and soothe your emotions. Some people attribute this to its connection with the greenness of nature and your affiliation with the natural world. Wear something green today or take a walk in nature.

Using imagery is the art of employing the mind to have an effect on the body. For example, are you feeling stressed right now? If so, try the following exercise:

Close your eyes and try to imagine what your stress looks like. Does it resemble a twisted rope, hardened wax or crashing waves? To move into a state of relaxation, start to imagine the rope untwisting, the hard wax melting or the crashing waves transforming into a calm sea.

day **85** *What if?*

Instant calm

TEASE YOURSELF

If your 'what if' moments get on your nerves, try teasing yourself with ludicrous suggestions, such as 'What if the sky falls in tomorrow?'

Most worrying begins with the words 'what if'. These thoughts are usually accompanied by visual images of misfortune, for example, 'What if I say something silly?' may be accompanied by images of you being laughed at by a crowd of people. Maybe you suffered from this sort of behavior when you were a child, for example, in the school playground.

It can help if you turn your 'what if?' into 'so what if?' followed by a 'well then.' For example, 'What if I say something silly?' becomes 'So what if I say something silly?' followed by 'Well then, I might feel a bit awkward for a moment, but no one will really care.' Try turning your 'what if?' into 'so what if?' today. It takes the stress out of the moment and helps you to feel calmer.

A few minutes' peace and quiet can make all the difference when trying to reduce stress levels. And a calming compress on your forehead will certainly help you relax, mentally and physically.

Blend three drops of lavender oil with three drops of rosemary oil and add them to a small bowl of water. Lay a clean face flannel on the water and then remove it and squeeze it out.

Roll up the flannel and place it on your forehead. Either lie down or lie back in a comfy chair or sofa. Close your eyes and take several deep breaths while relaxing your body completely. Focus your mind on breathing slowly in and out. Breathe out all the tension and breathe in calmness.

Flower meditation

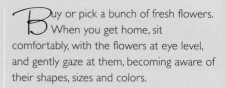

Buy or pick a bunch of fresh flowers. When you get home, sit comfortably, with the flowers at eye level, and gently gaze at them, becoming aware of their shapes, sizes and colors.

After a few minutes, close your eyes and visualize the flowers in your mind's eye. If the visualization becomes difficult, open your eyes and look at the flowers again. Then close your eyes and recreate a mental image of the flowers. You can expand this meditation to touching and smelling. Take a moment to reflect on the diversity and beauty of flowers in nature.

Release your jaw

Tension is frequently held in the jaw and sometimes this causes your jaw to become clamped and achy and your teeth to be clenched. Try this simple exercise to release it again.

Slowly open your mouth as wide as possible. Close it again. Repeat this opening and closing movement for about two minutes. Lightly press your fist under your chin and open your mouth, pressing your jaw downward against your fist. Maintain this pressure for about a minute. If you grind your teeth while you sleep, practice this exercise before you go to bed.

Instant calm

FACIAL YOGA

If yoga is good for your body, think about how good it would be for your face! Keep your facial muscles moving as much as you can and give all of your face regular chances to move as much as possible. This way you'll keep flexible and supple – facially!

Are you one of those people who's often impatient or constantly 'on the go'? Are you continually rushing through your life, which is overflowing with commitments?

The Australian Bush Essence, black-eyed Susan, will enable you to slow down, to reach that still center within and find calm. Put a few drops into a bottle of water and sip throughout the day.

Increase your magnesium

Magnesium is the fourth-most abundant mineral in the body and is essential for maintaining good health. If you don't have enough of it in your body, this could cause increased levels of adrenaline, which can lead to a feeling of anxiety. If you take the contraceptive pill or are under a lot of stress, you need more magnesium than usual.

To get the richest sources, eat green leafy vegetables, nuts, sesame seeds, wholegrain bread, fish, meat and dairy foods. Coffee inhibits the absorption of magnesium, so make sure you don't wash this supplement down with it!

Balls beneath your feet

This calming exercise will give your feet a workout and also press on some reflexology points. Reflexology is a gentle healing therapy, whereby you use pressure techniques on the hands and feet, which in turn affect other parts of the body.

Try this simple calming exercise. Place a tennis ball beneath the arch of your bare foot and, with a comfortable downward pressure, move your foot back and forth, so that the ball moves from the toes to the heel. Do this for two minutes on your right foot, then two minutes on your left foot.

Instant calm

INSTANT HAND REFLEXOLOGY

Take an ordinary golf ball and roll it gently around the palms of your hands. This action benefits several reflex areas at once.

Kunzite crystal is an excellent stone to use when you need to ground and calm yourself. It promotes feelings of peace, inner strength and relaxation. If you're the kind of person who swings between depression and elation, kunzite can help stabilize you; it actually contains lithium, which is used in psychiatry to control bi-polar disorders.

Keep a piece of kunzite near you during your day. You can wear it as a piece of jewelry, but it is also good to hold it when you are meditating. Alternatively, you can use it as a pendulum for dowsing.

Instant calm

KUNZITE QUALITIES
Think of the positive properties of kunzite and how they might help you:
• Spirituality
• Communication
• Peace
• Connection to universal love.

Whether you tried out several ideas this month or just one, you might like to reflect on what you chose to try and why, and if it worked for you.

1. How many activities did you try this month?
- 1–3 activities ☐
- 4–10 activities ☐
- 11–20 activities ☐
- 20–31 activities ☐

2. How many did you repeat several times in the month?
- 1–3 activities ☐
- 4–10 activities ☐
- 11–20 activities ☐
- 20–31 activities ☐

3. Which activities had a positive effect on your mood this month?
Use the page opposite to make notes about what worked for you and what didn't.

Notes, jottings and thoughts

When was the last time you had a really good shout? Believe it or not, shouting can be very good for you, helping you to release tension.

You don't need to shout at anyone in particular, but just in general, just for the hell of releasing energy that has nowhere to go. Never tried it? Well, here's your chance. Go somewhere in the countryside on your own, sit in the car (windows wound up) and yell your head off. If you're not in a car, go somewhere remote, where there is no one else around.

Wandering around a museum or art exhibition can be very soothing. The slow pace and interesting artefacts distract you and absorb your attention.

Take the time to read about the artist, the pictures and perhaps take a guided tour so you are better informed about what you are looking at. Sit down for a while and contemplate one of the pieces. Look at it in detail and let your mind wander. Admire the colors, the composition, the detail, the technique, the thinking behind it. Absorb as much as you can and learn something new and unexpected. You will be surprised how calming this activity is.

Don't forget to stop off in a café afterwards to reflect and refresh.

Instant calm

TAKE YOUR NOTEBOOK

While you are visiting an exhibition, take the time to sketch small details in a notebook or make notes about what you are observing, so that you can look back at them later.

Dissolve into the Earth

Try this exercise to calm and ground yourself. You simply lie on the ground and let yourself 'dissolve' into it. Allow yourself to experience being a part of the Earth. Don't make any effort to do this; just let it happen. Dissolving like this will bring you a sense of calm and serenity, recharging your energy.

When you have dissolved and really sunk into the Earth, allow yourself to feel cherished, calmed and strengthened.

Instant calm

....

VISUALIZE DISSOLVING

Think of an ice cream or sorbet gradually melting on your tongue.

warm towel on your face is great for helping you to relax. No wonder this is common in traditional barbers' shops.

If you want to try the same thing at home to calm down after a hectic day (and this isn't a male preserve!), all you have to do is soak a small, clean towel in warm-to-hot water and wring it out. Lie down in a quiet place, close your eyes and put the hot towel over your face. For an extra-relaxing treat, you could add a few drops of lavender oil to the water before you soak the towel.

Instant calm

CUCUMBER CALM
For a quick, calming stress relief, cut two thin slices of cucumber and place them over your closed eyes. Notice how cool and restful they are. Lie still and think about the word 'calm' for at least ten minutes.

Palm to calm

Palming helps you rest your eyes and calm your mind. Cover your closed eyes with your hands, making sure there is no pressure on your eyeballs. The palms of your hands are slightly cupped over each eye, with the fingers loosely interlaced on your forehead.

There should be no light, or as little as possible, entering your eyes. Once you are palming, open your eyes and look around to see if you can adjust your hands to exclude as much light as possible. Close your eyes and focus on deepening your breath for maximum relaxation.

The calm diet

Have you ever heard the cliché 'You are what you eat'? It's so true. So it follows that improving your diet will not only enhance your health, but also calm your mind down.

Try to avoid or limit stimulating foods that heighten your mental activity, such as too many hot spices, processed foods, vinegar, onion, radishes, garlic, preservatives, cola, coffee and tea. Calming foods that are easy to digest and provide high energy include herbs, fruit, vegetables, milk and milk products, nuts and seeds, grains and beans.

Music to chill by

Instant calm

CALMING COMMUTE

Put calming classical music on your I-pod and play it while you are in potentially stressful situations such as on a busy train or bus or waiting at the dentist's surgery.

When you are choosing music to help you feel calm, use the following guidelines. Choose music that has flowing melodies rather than fragmented and disjointed chords. Select music with a low pitch and slow tempo. The higher the frequency of sound or pitch, the more likely it will be to irritate you.

Try using sounds from nature such as ocean waves. Experiment with New Age and 'space' music. Classical music marked *adagio* and *largo* are highly effective. You can enjoy music to calm and soothe you anywhere and any time.

Eat mindfully

Mindfulness is a supremely calming state. This is when we are fully living in the present moment, with no thoughts of the past or the future. We are just in the 'now'.

Try this exercise when you are eating something ordinary like an apple. Sit down with the apple in your hands and look at it in depth, noting its color and texture. Smell the apple. Feel it. Allow yourself time to notice and absorb it. Then bring it to your mouth, being aware of your saliva increasing. Really bring all your senses into play as you slowly bite into it. Let the chunk stay in your mouth before you slowly chew and swallow it. Notice what happens in your mouth and throat. Look at the bitten apple in your hand, seeing all its nuances of shape, color and texture.

Instant calm

THINK 'APPLE'
After you have tried out the apple visualization (see left), let it stay with you. Whenever you feel the need to calm down, think 'apple' and you will be reminded of your calming visualization.

YOUR JOURNAL

Carry your journal or notebook around with you. Choose one that is easy to put in your bag and which you like as an object. Use odd spare moments to write in it; whenever you feel like expressing yourself.

Writing in a regular journal is a remarkable way of easing your worries and nurturing your spirit. It harnesses your power to tap into layers of the subconscious mind, while it has the ability to zap the nervous, passive energy that leads to worry.

If you are stuck and have nothing concrete to write about, try recording snippets of conversations you overhear: facts, feelings, fantasies, descriptions, impressions, quotes, images and ideas. Draw pictures to illustrate your words. Externalizing your thoughts and feelings invariably leads to a calmer you.

Commune with nature

There's nothing quite so grounding or calming as communing with nature. Try hugging a tree, standing barefoot on grass or putting your hands into sand, soil or running water. If this isn't possible, listen to a CD of nature sounds or look at a glossy book full of fantastic nature photography.

Help others

Who was the last person you helped? What did you do? How did this act make you feel? Often you will find that helping others lets you help yourself. The act of kindness removes us from our own neediness into someone else's sphere of need. Today, help a neighbor, friend or a stranger.

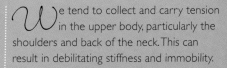

We tend to collect and carry tension in the upper body, particularly the shoulders and back of the neck. This can result in debilitating stiffness and immobility.

To release tension in your shoulders, try this straightforward exercise. Tighten the muscles in your shoulders by pulling them upward and forward. Hold them as tight as you can for ten seconds and then relax them. Now, tighten the muscles in your shoulders by pulling them back tight for ten seconds and then relaxing them. Breathe deeply and exhale completely.

If you're feeling vulnerable and ill at ease, visualize a huge gold and silver egg surrounding you, protecting you on all sides and both above and below. Now imagine painting the inside of the egg with a protective layer of blue. You are totally safe and cocooned within this egg.

This beautiful golden space protects you from anything negative outside of you. However, it allows your own light and love to radiate out of it. Hold on to this image until you feel a sense of calmness and serenity filling all the muscles, organs and cells of your body.

Instant calm

CALMING EGG
Place a ceramic, stone or wooden egg on your desk. When you need to be reminded of your egg visualization (see left) to make yourself feel safe and calm, look at it with a soft gaze for five minutes.

Give a little love

THINK OF SOMEONE

If someone you love pops into your mind, send them a postcard or a pretty greetings card just because you were thinking of them.

Sometimes we can get so caught up in our own lives and problems that we forget about other people. When we give to others, through simple actions, we come out of ourselves and consider the world beyond.

So if you're having a bad day today, remember this and phone someone or arrange to meet them and concentrate on asking them about their life, their goals and aspirations. Get out of yourself by taking an interest in someone else's life. Give a little love and genuinely be there for them. See how good it makes you feel.

Feeling stressed? The herb passiflora, which has a long history of use in teas and infusions to help insomnia, is an excellent remedy for anxiety and stress. It is also useful for headaches and PMS.

To make a passiflora tea, steep a teaspoonful of the herb with boiling water for ten to 15 minutes and drink it two to three times per day. Alternatively, you can take a few drops of passion flower tincture three to four times per day. You can combine passiflora with valerian and lemon balm for their sedative properties.

117

AFFIRMATION
Repeat your chosen affirmations several times throughout the course of the day.

Affirmation is the technique of auto-suggestion, whereby you repeat words or phrases to yourself to influence your subconscious, which in turn affects the way you behave. It is important to word affirmations in the present moment and include simple, active, positive words such as 'I feel calm.'

Identify how you want to feel and then use that word (for example use 'calm', which you aspire to, and not what you don't want to feel, for example, panicky). Use the 'I' word as much as possible. For example, 'I feel relaxed and I want to own the affirmation.'

Try time management

Being able to manage your time is a vital skill, helping you to take control of your life and feel calm. Here are some useful tips to help you achieve this:

- Say 'no'. If today is fully loaded, and you have lots of tasks that need your attention, refuse to take on any additional tasks, responsibilities or unnecessary distractions.
- Prioritize. Focus on your 'to do' list first, before doing other, less important, things.
- Delegate. Don't sweat the small stuff. We can't get involved with everything that claims our attention. Let go of things that can be passed on to others. You can also show others how to do part of your work, so you can focus on the things that only you can do.

Perfect Pilates

The central philosophy of Pilates, the highly acclaimed exercise and bodywork system, is to strengthen the core postural muscles and develop balanced alignment through the use of slow, controlled movements and breathing. Its overall effect is supremely calming.

Try the Neutral Spine exercise. Lie on your back with your arms by your sides. Your knees are bent and your legs and feet are parallel to each other, about hip-width apart. Inhale. Exhale and use your abs to press your lower spine into the floor. Inhale to release. Exhale and pull your lower spine up, creating a small arch in the low back. Inhale to release.

Island of peace

Today, take a few moments to try out this superbly calming visualization. Sit or lie down. Close your eyes and breathe deeply, imagining all your worries drifting gently away. Visualize your own island of peace, where you can go at any time when you need to rejuvenate. Rhythmic waves are gently splashing near your bare feet and the water reflects the clear blue sky and gold glimmers of the sun's rays.

Feel the sun's heat on your body and the dry, soft sands beneath your feet. Step into the surf and feel the cool wet sand oozing between your toes. Feel the breeze drying you off. Imagine walking with a carefree stride. You are very relaxed, breathing deeply and looking out to the distant horizon. You feel completely calm and at peace.

Watch a soap

People often sneer at television soaps, but watching your favorite with a hot drink and your feet up on the sofa can be a happily mind-numbing experience, helping you to forget your cares for a short while. It allows time for switch-off and escape; essential for your overall calmness.

You can immerse yourself in a sort of parallel universe. The characters seem real and it's like having a window into someone else's life, but without all the hassle. The characters are familiar; you can criticize them, commiserate with them (in your head), cry and laugh with them, but without commitment.

Blissed-out orgasm

Sex is more than a hormonal discharge and momentary pleasure. If you're feeling stressed out, having an orgasm can take the edge off and set you on the route to calmness again.

There is increased blood flow from sexual stimulation, which comes to a relaxing climax with an orgasm. The tension in your body dissipates and the pent-up nervous energy in your system is dispersed. The end result? You feel calm and even full of bliss. It's a relaxation of your whole body and its muscles, all at once.

Relaxing bath bag

When you take the time to have a long, relaxing bath, make the most of its calming effects by using a fragrant bath bag. Place 30 g (1oz) each of lavender flowers, peppermint, chamomile flowers and lemon balm in a muslin bag, tie it tightly closed and hook it over your hot-water tap.

Allow the water to run through it as your bath fills up. Step into the soothing bath and lie down with your eyes closed. Relax completely for ten minutes before starting your cleansing or beauty regime.

Hassled and fed up with cooking after a long day at work? If you feel you really need to relax at the end of a busy day, plan a take-away meal.

You can order most types of cuisine to be delivered right to your door. There's a vast range of take-aways, in any style you care to think of. Choose from good old fish and chips, burgers, sandwiches to more exotic curries, Chinese dishes and Thai food, all delivered piping hot, without you having to do more than use your dialling finger.

Now curl up with a glass of wine and wait for the doorbell to ring.

There's nothing like a warming bowl of soup on a cold day to calm you down. It's true comfort food. This carbohydrate-rich snack helps your brain release serotonin, the feel-good chemical that also reduces anxiety.

Heat olive oil in a large pan and soften a chopped onion for ten minutes. Add two cloves of crushed garlic, cook for a further minute before stirring in some rosemary and two tablespoons of tomato purée. Stir for another minute then add 198 g (7 oz) dried cannellini beans (soaked overnight in 1.4 litres/6 cups water) together with the soaking water. Simmer for an hour before seasoning and blending half of the soup. Return everything to the pan, add 110 g (3½ oz) macaroni and cook for ten to 12 minutes.

A refreshing sleep leaves you ready for action and you can tackle the next day with a calm approach.

Here are some tips to help you get a good night's sleep:

- Avoid drinking stimulants such as caffeine.
- Use the bed for sleeping (don't watch TV or use a laptop in bed).
- Don't have bright lights on around your home before you retire to bed.
- Don't exercise when bedtime's coming up soon.
- Don't go to bed hungry.
- If you wake up in the night, avoid looking at the clock.
- Keep your bedroom at a comfortable temperature.
- If you have problems with noise use a white noise generator.

Instant calm

MINI-NAPS
Take a mini-nap after lunch, before you start work again. Just close your eyes for ten minutes. Don't worry about actually dropping off to sleep. Just relax.

day 118 | *Get philosophical*

Take time today to muse on the purpose of your life; where you are going and whether there's a 'divine plan' for you. Don't allow yourself to become cynical; be open to the possibility that there may be answers. Your goal is to develop a personal philosophy that can sustain and nourish you.

day 119 | *Go to the movies*

Going to the movies is a welcome escape. It allows you to be somewhere else and experience a cathartic range of emotions. Remember a film that moved you or inspired you and how much calmer you felt afterwards. If you don't feel like going out, treat yourself to a DVD and some popcorn.

The yogic Child Pose is soothing and relaxing, gently stretching your back muscles, releasing pressure from the spine and bringing blood to the brain.

Sit on your heels, knees and feet together, with the tops of your ankles flat on the floor. Let your hands relax at your sides. Inhale, and, as you exhale, bend forward from your hips, placing your chest on your thighs, your forehead on the floor, and your hands, palms up, near your feet. Don't round your back; elongate your spine while holding the posture by reaching toward your kneecaps with your chest. Hold and relax completely.

An anchor is a nervous system cue that elicits from memory sensations of calmness. These are useful tools you can use at any time.

Sit in a quiet place, eyes closed. Focus on your breathing and your body. Become aware of your heart area. When you notice your attention wandering, return it to the centre of love and warmth in your chest.

Imagine yourself in the past, when you felt safe and calm. Recall this time in detail, developing every aspect of calmness. At the peak moment of your image, make a unique sensory signal (for example, put your thumb against the second knuckle of your index finger) and form a mental picture of yourself in a state of calmness. This signal becomes your personal anchor. If you feel agitated, trigger your anchor.

Choose a base oil such as sweet almond oil or jojoba in which to blend your essential oils.

Fill a small bottle with the base oil and use two drops of clary sage, four drops of cedarwood essence, two drops of mandarin essence and one drop of grapefruit essence.

Dab this mixture on the inside of your wrist and behind your ear for instant calm.

checklist 4 *How did you do?*

Whether you tried out several ideas this month or just one, you might like to reflect on what you chose to try and why, and if it worked for you.

1. How many activities did you try this month?

- 1–3 activities ☐
- 4–10 activities ☐
- 11–20 activities ☐
- 20–30 activities ☐

2. How many did you repeat several times in the month?

- 1–3 activities ☐
- 4–10 activities ☐
- 11–20 activities ☐
- 20–30 activities ☐

3. Which activities had a positive effect on your mood this month?

Use the page opposite to make notes about what worked for you and what didn't.

Notes, jottings and thoughts

day 123 | *Nurture yourself*

Instant calm

CONTEMPLATE 'NURTURE'
Meditate on this word and see where its associations take you.

Ask yourself 'How do I nurture myself?' Take a sheet of paper and divide it into three headings:

1. Nurturing people.
2. Nurturing places and things.
3. Nurturing activities.

In each column list the items that fit into that category. You can then try taking one thing from each column each day and engaging with it as fully as you can. This activity will help you to increase your feelings of calmness and comfort associated with these people, places, things and activities.

The sivananda yoga training system aims to retain the vitality of the body. Try the Seated Forward Bend. Sit on the floor with your legs stretched out in front of you. Pull your toes back toward you. Sit tall, lift and lengthen through your spine. Stretch your arms toward the ceiling and breathe in. Hinge at the hips and extend forward, reaching out with your arms. Take hold of your toes (bend your knees slightly if necessary). With as straight a back as possible, keep extending over your legs while relaxing your neck and head. Stay in the extension for 30 seconds to one minute while focusing on a gentle breath. Concentrate on extending and not pulling down to avoid placing too much strain on your lower back.

Instant calm

THE YOGIC BREATH
When you are doing yoga poses, concentrate on your breath. This will carry you through.

135

Everyone experiences fear at times; this a normal emotion that helps you deal with danger. However, you might experience excessive fear, which becomes ongoing and distressing. The more you manage your fear, the sooner you'll feel calmer and be able to accomplish your goals. Here are some helpful tips:

- Raise the awareness of your fear so you know when to make changes.
- Accept the fear and stop beating yourself up for having it.
- Don't try to rationalize your fears.
- Put a limit on the fear and don't let it run wild.
- Call on your intuition for answers.
- Remove yourself from people or situations that induce fear.
- Ask for help.

Try this eye pillow for a really relaxing break. Take a piece of silk 12 × 50 cm (5 × 20 inches) or 25 × 25 cm (10 × 10 inches) plus one cup of flaxseed and half a cup of lavender buds. Fold the silk, right sides together. Stitch the silk together, leaving a small opening. Turn right sides out. Mix the flaxseed and buds together and fill the bag. Sew it closed. Lie down with the pillow over your closed eyes and chill out!

Instant calm

CALMING LAVENDER

Rub lavender essential oil on your wrist pulse points. Enjoy!

137

Abdominal breathing

HAND ON BELLY
In times of stress, place
one hand gently on your
belly to reconnect with
your breath.

If you're feeling tense, this exercise will help to calm you. Find a quiet place, then lie or sit down and close your eyes. You're going to inhale through your nose and exhale through your mouth. Place your hands on your belly. As you inhale through your nose, push your belly up, feeling it rise. Rest a beat, before exhaling slowly through your mouth, feeling your belly go down. Repeat this cycle five times.

Now place your hands under the breast area on each side. As you inhale through your nose, expand your ribs and feel your hands push out. Rest a beat, before exhaling slowly through your mouth. Repeat this cycle five times. Now do a complete breathing cycle, inhaling for a count of five from your belly and ribcage and exhaling completely for a count of six. Repeat this cycle five times.

Also known as 'eleuthero', Siberian ginseng has been used for centuries in Eastern countries, including China and Russia. You can take Siberian ginseng as liquid extracts, solid extracts, powders, capsules, and tablets, and as dried or cut root for tea.

For long-term conditions, such as fatigue or stress, you can take the ginseng for three months, followed by two to three weeks off.

Be sure to consult a herbalist before you start taking it.

Ginseng quietens the spirits, stabilizes the soul, invigorates the body and prolongs life.

Chinese medical text, Shen Nung, 20 BC

Fly above it all

If life is overwhelming you, sit down for a moment and close your eyes. Imagine you're a bird flying high in the sky looking down on the little houses, the miniature people and the world below. All around you is space and freedom. Swoop and glide on the currents of cool air high up here away from it all. Take some deep breaths and feel yourself gradually calming down. When you're ready, open your eyes and enjoy the rest of your day.

When you are under stress, you may feel that things are happening too fast. A technique, called 'slow-down breathing', can help you to settle down and feel more in control. It starts with abdominal breathing (see page 138) and uses cue words to help you focus and clear your mind.

Examples of cue words are 'calm' and 'safe.' As you inhale, silently say 'CALM'. As you exhale, silently say 'SAFE'. As you inhale, silently say 'PRESENT'. As you exhale, silently say 'NOW'. Practice these breathing techniques for five or ten minutes until you get the feel of them, then again several times a day (just for a few moments each time).

Instant calm

MINI-TRANQUILIZER
Practice slow-down breathing (see left) so that it is instantly ready to use as a mini-tranquilizer whenever you start feeling tense.

day 131 — *Make bread*

Instant calm

KNEADING
To get rid of some aggression, knead dough. If you're not baking, use play dough.

aking bread is a remarkably relaxing activity. Try this rosemary and garlic bread. Turn your oven on to 50°C (122°F). Take 500 g (18 oz) of plain flour and 2 teaspoons of dried yeast and mix them together. Add two cups of warm water, mixing all the time. Knead until the dough is fairly smooth, place it on an oiled baking tin and flatten out to fill it (this makes lovely flattish bread). Mix a little olive oil with some rosemary, a touch of garlic and sea salt and spread over the bread.

Put your bread in the oven, turning it up to 190°C (375°F). The bread will continue rising as the heat increases. Bake for about 25 minutes. Top with sesame seeds.

Blue jade for serenity

For a peaceful and passive energy source, try beautiful jade. Holding it and meditating will help you to relax and gain an inner serenity. If you are feeling restricted or overcome by situations beyond your control, keep a piece of this crystal near your bed.

Bathe in a wave

Bathe in a wave of relaxation. Consciously sweep it through your body. Imagine that you're standing under a waterfall that is washing away all your tension. Afterward you will be left feeling free and cleansed.

day 134 — Listen to a self-help CD

While you are lying down and coming into a state of relaxation, you may find it helpful to use a self-help CD. A soothing voice or some tranquil, gentle music will gently help you to achieve a state of relaxation.

There are many types of self-help CD available, but those that help you to visualize or meditate are probably the ones to go for. They combine a state of deep relaxation with constructive self-help suggestions, which will enable you to recharge your batteries and open your mind to all the positive ways you can use to help yourself.

Rhodiola rosea is used as a tonic to promote resistance to stress of all kinds. In modern times rhodiola rosea has come to be classified as an 'adaptogen'. Adaptogens are groups of medicinal herbs, which through various mechanisms, improve your body's ability to resist stress, essentially helping it to adapt physiologically.

Be sure to consult a herbalist before taking an adaptogen.

PLAY TIME
Whenever you feel the need of some calm in your day, pick up your musical instrument.

Some of us have never had the opportunity to learn to play a musical instrument. But playing can be highly creative and also relaxing.

What about learning the piano, tuba, clarinet or guitar? You'll gain satisfaction, confidence, and, most of all, calm.

Hops are the flowers of a vine that is native to North America, Asia and Europe and they can have a calming effect on the body. They have been used for centuries for their sedative qualities to help promote positive support for insomnia, anxiety and tension.

Hops are often combined with valerian root, passiflora and German chamomile in herbal preparations, in order to bolster their effects. You could use them as a dry herb in a bath, as a supplement or as a tea extract.

Be sure to consult a herbalist before you start taking them.

Gelsimium for apprehension

The homeopathic remedy gelsimium is helpful if you suffer from stage-fright about making a public performance or attending an interview, or if you feel anxious before a test, a visit to the dentist, or any other stressful event.

Gelsimium is thought to relieve anxiety in the form of apprehension about particular events, as well as generalized anxiety. The 30c formulation is recommended, taken as you need it, up to three or four times daily, for no longer than one week.

Don't sweat the small stuff...and it's all small stuff.

Richard Carlson

Baked figs

Figs are filled with potassium, which should sort you out if you're feeling irritable after a bad day.

Try this simple recipe. Preheat the oven to 200°C (392°F) and smear olive oil on the base of a baking dish. Snip off the stalks and cut two figs in half, place in a dish (cut side up) and sprinkle with lemon juice and demerara sugar. Bake for 15 minutes, then baste and sprinkle over the remaining sugar before baking for a further five minutes. Put a dollop of cream on top to really help you feel calm.

Drawing for relaxation

Why not try drawing a picture of your tension? This might be an abstract design, a doodle or a symbolic picture of yourself in a state of tension. Let your drawing tell you how it feels, what's causing it, and what you can do about it.

Close your eyes, take a deep breath and relax. Now draw a picture of relaxation. It can be an abstract design, a doodle, or a picture of yourself being relaxed. This activity increases your awareness of the difference between relaxation and tension.
(Adapted from *The Creative Journal* by Lucia Capacchione)

Try this calming meditation anywhere. Sit in a comfortable position and close your eyes. Take a few deep breaths and relax your body. Notice any sounds in your surroundings without thinking about them.

If you catch yourself thinking about a sound or about something else, then bring yourself back to listening. Notice how a sound comes into your awareness and then disappears again. Even sounds that continue for a long time are never exactly the same from one moment to the next. Every sound is unique and of the moment. Listening to the sounds that arise in each moment keeps you noticing and allowing the moment to be just the way it is.

A touch of retail therapy can soothe a troubled spirit, but don't get into debt for it, otherwise your troubled spirit might end up being even more troubled! If you're feeling down or stressed, take a couple of hours out to wander round the shops. You'll find it takes you out of yourself. Even if you just buy a lipstick or a bunch of flowers, you can calm yourself down and cheer yourself up.

Stress is not what happens to us. It's our response to what happens. And response is something we can choose.

Maureen Killoran

Walk on the beach

Apart from the beautiful view of the ocean and the exercise you'll get, there are many appealing aspects to a walk on the beach, winter or summer. Whatever the weather, try making a small collection of unusual or appealing things. Don't forget to stop and pick up a pretty shell, a piece of sea glass or an interesting chunk of driftwood. Watch the surf rolling hypnotically in and out and notice the always-changing colors of the water and sky.

In your journal, list the things you've seen that you are most drawn to. Write what they mean to you and why.

Instant calm

BEACH THINGS

- Shells
- Driftwood
- Waves
- Sunsets
- Sea glass
- Pebbles
- Seaweed
- Sand

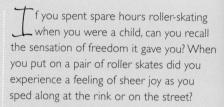

If you spent spare hours roller-skating when you were a child, can you recall the sensation of freedom it gave you? When you put on a pair of roller skates did you experience a feeling of sheer joy as you sped along at the rink or on the street?

Why not rediscover those sensations now? As an adult, skating can be such enormous fun plus it's a great way to de-stress and keep fit, too. Don't forget to try ice-skating as well. It's a seasonal thrill for all ages.

One of the deepest beliefs you carry is that you can control other people. You learn this belief by observing your parents or teachers in their attempts to control others.

The moment you become stressed with someone it means that you are trying to control them. However, when others sense you are trying to control them, up go the barriers and down goes your capacity to influence them.

The truth is, the more you try to control others, the less influence you have over them, whereas the less you attempt to control others, the more influence you will have and the calmer you will feel.

Today's thought

CONTROL
Who are you trying to control today?

To make a calming herbal bath bag, fill a square of cheesecloth with elder, jasmine, linden flowers and valerian root, tying it up with yarn. Place the bag in a bath partially filled with hot water. Steep for about 15 minutes, then fill as you normally do (remember that cooler baths are energizing while hot baths are enervating).

Keep the bag in the water during your bath to get maximum benefit, giving it an occasional squeeze. If you prefer a shower, use an herbal bag for a brisk rubdown.

Relaxation means releasing all concern and tension and letting the natural order of life flow through one's being.

Donald Curtis

These days our lives tend to be overcomplicated and this affects our stress levels. Clutter really does make us feel tense. So make the effort to prune and weed out all aspects of your life, whether in terms of possessions, commitments or people.

We tend to have too many things in our lives. So let go of possessions that do not enhance your life; things that take up space or make decision-making more complicated.

Identify what you are willing to take on to reach your goals and think about what you are willing to let go of. Identify activities that are all-consuming, but not necessarily important. Let go of relationships that do not enhance your life; people can be clutter, too!

Instant calm

MAKE A LIST
Today, make a list of ten things that bother you. Give yourself a month to fix or let go of them!

day 148 Have a at-home day

ake a full day off from work and don't bother to get dressed. Stay in your nightwear. Relax, stay comfortable, and do what you want. It'll feel like a mini-holiday and you won't even have to leave the house!

day 149 Count the positives

ow often do you count the positives in your life? Most people play down the good and focus on the bad. List all the good that has happened to you during the day. Acknowledge your achievements, as this will help to boost your confidence and make you feel calm.

Do some housework

Housework? Yes, I really did suggest do some housework! It's a great way to both clean your home and get fit. You can kill two birds with one stone!

Get the vacuum out, have a dust round and really get your body in gear. Repetitive, vigorous movements such as these can lull you into a near-meditative state, while the strenuous physical activity can actually release stress from your body. You will be rewarded with a cleaner living space and more soothing surroundings when you've finished. Results all round!

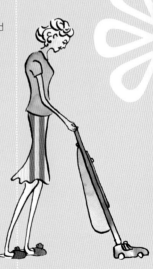

159

Have a DIY facial

Try giving yourself a calming facial today:

1. Cleanse your skin, applying circular motions from your neck upward.
2. Fill a bowl with hot water and add a couple of drops of lavender essential oil. Bend over the water with a tea towel over your head and breathe deeply.
3. With your exfoliater, gently massage your face with circular movements. Clean off.
4. Pop slices of cucumber or cold tea bags over your eyes while waiting for the mask to work. Wash off.
5. Massage your skin with an oil-based massage cream. Get some wheatgerm carrier oil, blend in either two drops of tea tree (oily skin) or two drops of neroli (sensitive skin). Shake. In sweeping motions apply from your neck up. Massage in with small circular movements.

Delegate today

day 152

Do you think of yourself as superhuman and able to do anything and everything? Delegating is a way of sharing the load and calming down your frenetic lifestyle. If someone else can do a task that you have lined up for yourself, then let them do it. Free yourself up to do something more pleasant, or better still, do nothing at all.

Take rest; a field that has rested gives a bountiful crop.

Ovid

Whether you tried out several ideas this month or just one, you might like to reflect on what you chose to try and why, and if it worked for you.

1. How many activities did you try this month?

- 1–3 activities ☐
- 4–10 activities ☐
- 11–20 activities ☐
- 20–30 activities ☐

2. How many did you repeat several times in the month?

- 1–3 activities ☐
- 4–10 activities ☐
- 11–20 activities ☐
- 20–30 activities ☐

3. Which activities had a positive effect on your mood this month?

Use the page opposite to make notes about what worked for you and what didn't.

Notes, jottings and thoughts

Chill with a manicure

The time to relax is when you don't have time for it.

Attributed to Jim Goodwin and Sydney J Harris

Attending to yourself can be deeply calming. Why not try giving yourself a manicure?

1. Strip old varnish off with acetone polish remover on a cotton ball.
2. Rest your hands in a bowl of warm water for five minutes. Add two tablespoons of liquid soap to soften the nails.
3. Apply cuticle oil or lotion on your dry hands to nourish and soften rough spots.
4. Use a cuticle stick to neaten your cuticles.
5. Exfoliate your hands with a mixture of olive oil and salt or raw sugar. Scrub for two to three minutes and then wash your hands thoroughly.
6. Dry your hands and apply a rich moisturizer.
7. Apply a base coat, and then two thin coats of polish. Finish with a top coat.

If you suffer from nervous tension, which is making you tense, why not try using skullcap as a mild sedative. It is commonly combined with valerian for insomnia. The herb is a member of the mint family and is a native of North America, where it thrives in moist woodlands.

Make a cup of skullcap tea by pouring 250 ml (one cup) of boiling water over 5–10 g (one to two teaspoons) of the dried herb and steeping for 10–15 minutes. You can drink this tea three times per day. Alternatively take a tincture made from fresh skullcap, 2 ml (half a teaspoon) three times per day.

The word 'mandala' is from the ancient Indian language Sanskrit. Loosely translated to mean 'circle', a mandala represents the concept of wholeness and is a symbol of the universe. It is usually used as a tool for meditation. Mandalas have a center, or axis, around which important and meaningful symbols, such as deities, are arranged.

The process of creating a mandala is a creative, soothing one and you'll find it helps you to become mindful and calm. You can create a mandala with colored pens, chalks or paints and paper. Start by tracing a circle around a plate. Then fill in the circle with color and form using any symbolism that is specially meaningful to you.

For a calm-down strategy to make you feel more relaxed try this. Stand and put your hand on your stomach. Close your eyes, relax and breathe normally. When you exhale, your stomach should let your hand move closer to your body. To breathe properly, make sure your shoulders aren't moving up and down. This is called diaphragmatic breathing. Now close your eyes, and begin counting breaths. Count each breath silently until you reach 11 and then start at one again. Keep doing this repeatedly, and if you lose count, start at one again.

Make empowering choices

'SHOULDS' AND 'OUGHTS'
Before you act, think about the words 'should' and 'ought'.

When you make meaningful choices in your life, you feel far more in control and therefore a great deal calmer in general. Do you make choices in your life, or do you live by 'shoulds' and 'oughts'?

Consider all the activities you are undertaking today. Which choices are you making because you want to and which choices are you making because you have responsibility for someone or something? And which choices are you making in order to please someone else, perhaps someone you are nervous of?

Fresh food is nutritionally best for developing a healthy body and mind. Ideally organic, vegetables, salads and fruit benefit us most as they have less harmful chemicals. Organic meat and fresh farmed fish is good because it contains fewer hormones. Preparing fresh food is a very calming activity and knowing that what you're eating is good for you is truly an added bonus.

aydreaming is a great way to stay calm in an intense situation. Take a five-minute breather from life and picture yourself relaxing, or picture an event in your life that was particularly positive or enjoyable. Doing this and then coming back to the reality of the present can help you to confront the situation better and deal with it head on.

Eating berries can help soothe your nerves when they're a bit frayed. Because the carbohydrates found naturally in berries turn to sugar very slowly, you won't suffer a blood sugar dip. Berries are also a good source of vitamin C, which helps reduce the stress hormone cortisol.

As a delicious serving suggestion, top a bowl of strawberries and raspberries with a dollop of crème fraîche and a sprinkling of chopped almonds.

Relaxation means releasing all concern and tension and letting the natural order of life flow through one's being.

Donald Curtis

day 161 — *Step out of denial*

Instant calm

MAKE A CHANGE TODAY

Pinpoint something simple that you could change in your life today.

Are you getting so used to stress that you expect it to be a regular part of your life? Do you complain about your life, but do nothing to change it?

Think on the following. What is the thing you're most afraid to say out loud about your life? What are you scared of happening to you? If you were run over and killed by a bus tomorrow, what would be your greatest regret? Maybe in order to get a sense of calm in your life, you need to wake up and change something.

Stretch in the shower

The hot water will loosen up your muscles, so it's easier to get a good stretch while you're in the shower. The act of stretching will help to release stored tension and enable you to start the day feeling calmer, more peaceful and ready to handle whatever comes your way.

Acknowledge reality

Face your causes of stress head-on. Don't try to deny them or wish that they hadn't happened. Think 'This is real. I can handle it. I'm finding the best possible way to cope right now.'

Begin this calming meditation by visualizing every in-breath to be a breath of white light. With each exhalation, see your breath as coming out as black smoke. This is all the negativity stored in your body. Imagine it coming out of your mouth and dissipating into the air.

Continue this cleansing breathing for a few minutes. Then visualize a clear, warm beam traveling into your body, coming down from above your head, passing through your body, then looping back around and coming back up your spine, enveloping your whole body with serenity.

Have a good cry

Humans are the only mammals who can shed tears of emotion. Did you know crying is really a form of stress-release? It is a natural and essential biological function resulting in the elimination of stress hormones.

When you feel pressure, frustration, sorrow or anger, any negative emotions, you could take effective measures to release them through crying. This is a natural, perfectly healthy way of releasing stress, so never feel bad about it.

Instant calm

SHED A TEAR
Don't hold back your tears, they are there to relieve you of stress.

Do the Easy Pose

For a truly calming exercise, try out the Easy (yoga) Pose. Sit cross-legged, with your hands on your knees, your back and head straight. While you are inhaling, raise your arms overhead, with the palms facing upward, and clasp your hands together above your head, stretching upward and feeling a pull in your spine and in the undersides of your arms.

Exhale and lower your arms with your palms facing down. Repeat this several times. Then, with your arms hanging at your sides, roll your shoulders forward, up to your ears, back to the center of your back and down several times. Then repeat the exercise in the opposite direction.

Put on a calm face

Conventional wisdom says that happiness triggers the act of smiling. But recent studies suggest that this process is actually a two-way street.

Smiling can contribute to feelings of happiness, and in a stressful situation it can help to keep you calm. Try smiling more and you'll soon see that you'll start to feel better.

Instant calm

PUT A SMILE ON YOUR FACE
Today, start getting into the habit of smiling whenever you think of it. It'll make a positive difference to all aspects of your life.

Neroli oil is a plant oil produced from the blossom of the bitter orange tree and neroli is considered to have a soothing effect on the nervous system.

Try making this lovely blend to use on your hands. Add three or four drops of the essential oil to one cup of sweet almond oil and two tablespoons of wheat-germ oil.

To fix the oil so that it is longer-lasting try adding grapefruit seed extract. And if you want to use the blend on children or pregnant women, just use half the quantity of essential oil.

A face mask is a great way to relax and beautify yourself at the same time. Try this deliciously perfumed face mask. Mix two teaspoonfuls of honey, two teaspoonfuls of sweet almond oil and three drops of rose essential oil. Now snip off the top of a vitamin E capsule and add it to the mixture. Massage it onto your clean face and neck using your fingertips. Relax for 15 minutes and then rinse off with lukewarm water. Gently pat yourself dry to reveal a fresh, soft complexion.

The more tranquil a man becomes, the greater is his success, his influence, his power for good. Calmness of mind is one of the beautiful jewels of wisdom.

James Allen

reating your feet with loving care feels very calming. When you get a spare moment try out this pampering foot bath. Put enough warm water in a bowl to cover your feet. Mix five drops of lavender or sandalwood essential oil with one dessertspoonful of apple cider vinegar and add to the bowl. The apple cider vinegar helps to disperse the oil and has therapeutic properties.

Alternatively you could mix the essential oil with some powdered milk and make it into a paste before mixing it with the water. This will help to disperse the oil. If you want to add an extra relaxing dimension to your footbath, you can place marbles or small pebbles at the bottom of the bath to run your feet over.

Bend and breathe

day **171**

To calm down and revitalize yourself, try this simple exercise. Stand with your feet slightly apart and stretch your arms up over your head as high as you comfortably can. As you raise your arms, inhale slowly until your lungs are full. Then bend forward at your waist, keeping your knees slightly bent, while you swing your arms down and back behind you.

As you bend forward, exhale quickly, emptying all the air from your lungs. Return to a standing position and inhale deeply as you stretch your arms back up over your head again. Repeat this exercise several times to stimulate the flow of chi (a term in Traditional Chinese Medicine meaning energy). This procedure also helps to loosen tense muscles.

Take some dog rose

If you are feeling fearful, the Bush Flower Essence dog rose might calm you down. This essence is helpful for overcoming your fear, because it allows an increase in the flow of chi (body energy).

It also works on the spleen, which in Traditional Chinese Medicine helps you to absorb the spiritual essence of your food, which is then taken to the pineal gland (third eye) to assist spiritual understanding for additional calmness.

Try neurolinguistic programing (NLP) to calm your mind. Picture your inner voice criticizing you and imagine where that is located in space. Is the voice behind you, to the left or right of you or in front of you? Become aware of how it speaks to you and how it sounds.

Now interrupt that thought pattern. Think of the critical voice. Imagine it being played backward. First do it fast and then slow, then hear it backward really fast. Do this three times. Now replace that backward voice with a new positive message. Give this positive message a calm, friendly voice. By interrupting the pattern and changing the structure, your mind is able to make you feel more relaxed.

There are few circumstances which so strongly distinguish the philosopher as the calmness with which he can reply to criticisms he may think undeservedly severe.

Charles Babbage

Use your peripheral vision

USE YOUR EYES
In odd spare moments, make a point of really looking at something, as though for the first time, like a child. You will start to notice things that you have never noticed before.

If you're feeling a little tense, using your peripheral vision will help to calm you. Find a point straight in front of you and focus on it. Now gradually become aware of what's around that point and let your vision spread out in front of you to the corners of the room, as your eyes continue to look at that point.

Let your awareness also spread behind you and let your senses of hearing, touch, smell and spatial awareness filter out to the periphery as well. Notice the positive changes in your physiological state.

Think pink

Have you ever wondered why little girls love pink so much? Perhaps it's because pink is a gentle and soothing color. It's nurturing, tender, protective and full of compassion. Why not try using it in your home or perhaps wear a little pink to promote positive and reassuring feelings.

When life gets you into a frazzle, take a few moments to consider your achievements. This will have the effect of calming you down and improving your self-confidence.

If you think that you don't have any achievements, think about all the things that you take for granted. Can you cook, read or ride a bicycle? Are you the organized one who keeps the family files, pays the bills and gets the kids to school? Take a little time to be proud of your achievements!

Even if you're not going anywhere special, put on your favorite outfit, polish your nails, put on a new shade of lipstick or do something different with your hair today. And then feel free to smile at yourself in the mirror before sharing that smile with the rest of the world! It's the fastest fix there is. You can't help but feel calmer when you're looking your best.

day 178 — *Wear an onyx necklace*

Onyx is a form of quartz and is said to absorb intense emotions, therefore leading to a sense of calmness. If you tend to live on the emotional or mental levels and struggle to maintain awareness of what is occurring around you, wearing an onyx necklace might help ground you.

day 179 — *Enjoy a neutral bath*

A neutral bath, in which you are immersed up to your neck in water slightly cooler than your body temperature, is great for soothing your emotional agitation. Soak in it for 20 minutes, adding water as needed to maintain the temperature of the bath.

If you're great to all your friends, why not be great to yourself, too? Are you too hard on yourself? Think of it this way: would you make an unpleasant remark to your best friend if she were having a bad day? No. So what would happen if you were your own friend? Would you be able to be more understanding and encouraging toward yourself?

Today, be that warm, supportive person for yourself! Stop working against your own wellbeing and be good to yourself instead! You'll soon find that your self-esteem soars and you'll discover that you feel calmer and happier with yourself and with the world around you, too.

*G*eopathic stress (GS) is the name given to natural or man-made energies emanating from the Earth, which can be detrimental to your health. Examples of things that cause GS are ley lines, underground water, foundations, sewage and water pipes.

If you are susceptible to geopathic stress, you may find it difficult to feel happy, energetic, emotionally stable and physically well. You can use a variety of methods such as muscle-testing, dowsing and intuition to locate the source and intensity of GS in your home or workplace.

Where you put your attention in your body has a big effect on how you feel. So pay attention to a special point in your body. It's located slightly below your navel and halfway between the your front and your back; in the very center of your body. At the same time look straight ahead and go into peripheral vision. Let your body relax. You can maintain this focus on your central point all the time, whatever you are doing. If you're really focused on this point, your body can't feel anxiety.

Instant calm

CALMING SNACK
You'll find that eating a banana (not too ripe) will help to calm you down at any time.

checklist 6 *How did you do?*

Whether you tried out several ideas this month or just one, you might like to reflect on what you chose to try and why, and if it worked for you.

1. How many activities did you try this month?

- 1–3 activities ☐
- 4–10 activities ☐
- 11–20 activities ☐
- 20–30 activities ☐

2. How many did you repeat several times in the month?

- 1–3 activities ☐
- 4–10 activities ☐
- 11–20 activities ☐
- 20–30 activities ☐

3. Which activities had a positive effect on your mood this month?

Use the page opposite to make notes about what worked for you and what didn't.

Notes, jottings and thoughts

Bore yourself to sleep

A stressful day may stop you falling asleep as easily as you would like. If this happens, try 'boring' yourself to sleep. This sounds a bit strange, but it can be very effective. It doesn't mean counting sheep.

Try thinking of something that bores you (this could be a TV program that fails to hold your interest, or a person who says tedious things all the time). The idea is to occupy your brain by preventing your worries from creeping into your thoughts.

Try out a DIY body wrap. You'll find it can help calm your frazzled nerves (you may need to ask a friend to help you with this).

Wrap your whole body in a cold, wet sheet and then cover yourself with a wool blanket. Keep your feet warm with blankets or a hot footbath. Leave the wrap on until your body heat has dried the sheet (the temperature is now neutral). This should take around 30 minutes. Once you have removed it, it will encourage you to relax and sleep.

day 185 — *Improve personal power*

Instant calm

SIMPLE SELF-EMPOWERMENT

Try these ideas:

- Change your route to work.
- Eat your meals at slightly different times.
- Stop watching TV at certain times.
- Restart an abandoned hobby or occupation.

Have you noticed how you tend to become agitated when you feel powerless? The definition of personal empowerment starts with a thought process whereby you feel secure in yourself: you feel as if you have power over your own life; you aren't at the mercy of events, but instead can have an impact on what happens to, or around, you.

A simple example of how you can exercise personal power is by changing a deeply entrenched habit. You could try starting up an exercise routine, or rethinking the way you react to a person who seems to constantly press your buttons.

Do you have enough fun in your life? It's a lot easier to have a little fun if there are children around (either yours or someone else's). You have to make an effort to be playful with them. If you can do this you'll notice that this light-hearted interaction can change your state of mind quite dramatically.

Think about the way you relate to kids. Do you really play with them, or do you just supervise them or expect them to keep themselves amused? Rolling on the ground with them, kneading play dough, or finger-painting a masterpiece with them can be a great diversion from your personal worries, and the children will love it, of course.

Visualize a calm person

Visualization is the art of creating a mental image that is similar to a visual perception. Next time you feel agitated, sit or lie down, close your eyes and take a few deep breaths. Visualize yourself as the chilled-out person you strive to be. See yourself as standing tall, physically relaxed and calm. You are dealing with the situation easily. You can manage any problems with confidence and still remain calm. Visualizing yourself as a calm person will help you to become a calmer person on a daily basis.

When you are experiencing a stress headache try out this ultra-simple technique. Fill a sink with the hottest water you can stand, and place your hands in it. Keep them there. As the water cools down, replace it with more hot water and keep your hands in for several minutes. The theory is that your blood rushes to your hands and away from your head, thus relieving your headache.

day 189 — Take a hike

One of the simplest ways to reduce stress is to take a long, hard hike. You'll find that the combination of challenging, strenuous exercise and the change of scenery and fresh air all combine to take you out of yourself and put the rest of your life into perspective.

Put on some comfortable clothes and supportive shoes, then head out. You don't have to live near hills and mountains to go for a serious walk. In the warmer months you can check out a city park and at colder times you might consider becoming a mall-walker. Go with whichever option is the most convenient and the most calming for your nerves.

Instant calm

PLACES TO WALK
Try the following venues:
• A large shopping mall
• A city park
• A new neighborhood
• A national park

A little nostalgia is so good for you and it can have a remarkably calming effect. Perhaps you have nostalgic feelings for Pac-Man. If so, why not try and track down some old video games that you liked when you were a child. There are places online where you can play them without downloading them. Or maybe you could find old games at a thrift shop.

Busy schedules don't always give you enough time to finish your meals in a leisurely fashion and this will add to your feelings of being stressed. You may have retained a few bad habits from rushed meals at school or heavy work schedules that only allow half an hour for lunch. So whenever you've got time to eat a meal without hurrying to get back to work or to meet an appointment, take advantage of it. It will be good for your digestive system and your nerves. Remind yourself that you don't have to hurry.

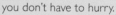

Don't procrastinate

Putting things off until the last minute may be adding to your stress. However, it's important to know yourself. You might be one of those who functions best under 'last-minute' pressure and stresses out when you start doing things too early. Sounds crazy, but it is true.

Forgive yourself

Life is not perfect and neither are you. Mistakes are made. Maybe you could have made better decisions, but what good does it do to dwell on it? Does it change the decision or the outcome? Nope. Forgive yourself and let it go!

Calmness is the cradle of power.

J G Holland

If you like walking, you'll find that it releases stress as well as being excellent exercise. Take as many opportunities to walk during your day as you can. Try setting a target of taking 10,000 steps a day, or whatever works best for you.

If you don't reach your target one day, you can carry over the rest until the next day, or forget about it and try again. You won't be answering to anyone but yourself and you will be walking off some of that stress.

Is there a possibility that you are stressed because you're overestimating your stressors? Maybe when you take a closer look you will realize that many of your stressors are really not that serious.

Once you become aware of this, you'll feel that you can deal with whatever the outcomes are. This means that your perception of the issues will fall into perspective and you can calm down.

Instant calm

JUST LOOK
Light a candle and gaze into it. You'll feel supremely calm.

This too will pass

When Abraham Lincoln was in the White House and experienced stress, he said to himself, 'This too shall pass.' He used this phrase as a kind of mantra to remind himself that the one constant in this universe is that everything changes. Say that phrase to yourself next time you feel upset. Some parts of your circumstances will change by themselves fairly quickly. Remind yourself that your feelings will change inevitably, even if you do nothing to change them. You won't stay upset forever. It's a simple idea and will ease the strain of the moment, creating less stress in your body, and making you a calmer person to interact with.

Have a jacket potato

day **197**

There are times when a little of what you fancy does you good, and this particularly applies to food. Maybe it's time for a feel-good snack and jacket potatoes are the kings of this snack category.

Put a potato in the oven or microwave. When it is almost ready, stir-fry 100 g (3½ oz) of turkey. Slice open the potato and mash a small amount of butter, sea salt and pepper into it. Top with half a cup of cottage cheese, turkey and chives.

> *If you are stressed by anything external, the pain is not due to the thing itself but to your own interpretation of it; and this you have the power to revoke at any time.*
>
> Marcus Aurelius

207

Sometimes it's great to make lists. Lists are effective, because you can see in tangible form all the things that you need to bring into focus, rather than letting them swim around in your mind. This is especially true when you make a list about how wonderful you are!

Are you nice? Thoughtful? Patient? Smart? Funny? Reliable? Caring? Keep your list handy and review it whenever you feel a bit down. You're special, so celebrate your unique qualities. Appreciate yourself!

Breathing using a yogic technique can be especially de-stressing and calming. Try this one. This technique helps to calm and balance your flow of chi and it's also a quick and easy cure for hiccups.

Sit quietly, with your back straight and your feet flat on the floor. Close your eyes and inhale slowly to a count of four. Hold your breath for a count of four. Then exhale slowly to a count of four. Repeat this breathing pattern three times.

The yogic Cat Stretch can be highly calming. Kneel on all-fours, tuck your chin toward your chest and curl your back up toward the ceiling. Hold this position for a few moments, and then slowly return to a flat-back posture. Exhale as you curl your back and inhale as you flatten it. Repeat these movements several times. As you stretch your body, you open up areas that may have become cramped by sitting at a desk all day and allow chi to flow more freely.

Qi Gung is the ancient Chinese energy-exercise system, which has long been used to help enhance calm. Try out this useful meditation.

In a quiet place, stand with your feet fairly close together. Let your arms drop at your sides and close your eyes. Relax your face muscles and your shoulders. Relax your chest and the front part of your body. Feel how natural your breathing is. Relax your back and feel all the muscles loosen. Relax your upper limbs right down to the fingertips. Relax your lower limbs right down to your toes. Feel all your tension running out of the soles of your feet. After you have relaxed your whole body, relax mentally. Feel that you do not have a care in the world, nor a thought in your mind.

The cyclone drives its powers from a calm center. So does a person.

Norman Vincent Peale

211

Rose geranium massage

Rose geranium as a plant was introduced to European countries in the 17th century and has been highly valued ever since. The oil has a balancing effect on the nervous system and it can help to relieve anxiety, while lifting your spirits. The oil works well if you blend it with lavender and neroli in a massage oil.

Rose geranium should be avoided during pregnancy.

There are hand-reflexology techniques you can learn to apply to yourself in stressful situations. They'll help relieve your anxiety.

Grip your left index finger with your right hand and squeeze gently. Hold until you can feel your heart beat, then release it. Move to the middle finger and again squeeze gently until you can feel your pulse. Continue with the ring and little fingers and then move to your right hand.

If you are feeling stressed, you can try using this technique of releasing sound and noise to help you calm down.

Stand with your feet shoulder-width apart, your knees slightly bent and your hips centered, as though you're about to squat. Keep your body loose and comfortable, with your arms at your sides. Begin by taking a few cleansing breaths. Choose a word such as 'calm'. Chant the word aloud. Focus on nothing but repeating the word over and over again. Let the sound of the word vibrate through your entire body. It's important to roll the sound through your body so that you can clear out the tightness in your muscles.

Punch a pillow

If you're feeling overwrought, punching a pillow or a cushion is a great way to release excess energy. Get yourself into a safe space such as your bed or the couch. Sit with your feelings for a moment or two and then let rip. Punch until you're all punched out. You might want to have a good cry or shout as you punch. Just let it out. Then you will feel calmer.

The last of the human freedoms is to choose one's attitude in any given set of circumstances, to choose one's own way.

Viktor Frankl MD

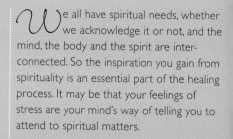

We all have spiritual needs, whether we acknowledge it or not, and the mind, the body and the spirit are interconnected. So the inspiration you gain from spirituality is an essential part of the healing process. It may be that your feelings of stress are your mind's way of telling you to attend to spiritual matters.

Making an overt connection with your spirit will provide healing for your mind and body.

Take a catnap

Having a short nap, or 'catnapping', can reduce the build-up of stress during the day and increase your alertness to help you deal with the rest of the day

Your nap should last between 15 and 20 minutes, giving your body a chance to recharge its batteries. The best time of day for napping is about eight hours after you wake up in the morning and eight hours before you go to bed at night.

day 208 Break it up

Take things one step at a time. It will help you break down anxiety. If wrapping a mountain of gifts, planning a project or unloading the dishwasher seems too hard (or dull), focus on achieving just one step of the process at a time.

day 209 Q-Tip it

Q-Tip is an acronym for 'Quit Taking It Personally!' This quick and easy stress-reduction technique can apply to the traffic jam, that extra few pounds you can't seem to lose, a bad-tempered boss, a frozen computer or your missing keys. Remind yourself to Q-Tip it!

Frankincense oil soothes and calms the mind, slowing down and deepening breathing. The word 'frankincense' comes from the French word 'Franc' meaning 'luxuriant' or 'real incense'.

Try using frankincense when you are meditating. If you put it into a burner, blended with sandalwood, frankincense will calm your mind, reduce anxiety and help you to feel an inner peace.

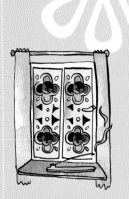

Change is a part of life and sometimes it's hard to take this on board. We all have dreams and goals, but you may realize that certain goals may no longer be attainable and that they may never become a reality.

If this is the case for you, accepting circumstances that cannot be changed can help you to focus on circumstances that you can alter.

Move toward your goals

day 212

People sometimes have dreams and goals that are not realistic and they waste time yearning for something that is never going to become a reality.

If this is you, now is the time to develop some goals that are really realistic. Sit down and compile a list of small steps you can take toward your goals. Perhaps doing something regularly, even if it seems like a small accomplishment, will enable you to do this. Instead of focusing on tasks that seem unachievable, ask yourself 'What's one thing I know I can accomplish today that will help me move in the direction I want to go?'

Whether you tried out several ideas this month or just one, you might like to reflect on what you chose to try and why, and if it worked for you.

1. How many activities did you try this month?

* 1–3 activities ☐
* 4–10 activities ☐
* 11–20 activities ☐
* 20–30 activities ☐

2. How many did you repeat several times in the month?

* 1–3 activities ☐
* 4–10 activities ☐
* 11–20 activities ☐
* 20–30 activities ☐

3. Which activities had a positive effect on your mood this month?

Use the page opposite to make notes about what worked for you and what didn't.

Notes, jottings and thoughts

The pursuit,
even of the best
things, ought to
be calm and
tranquil.

Marcus T Cicero

People under stress often have a hunched-over posture and a slightly hunched appearance; as though they are defending themselves against the world.

Maintaining good posture works a bit like smiling. If you make an effort to smile, you start to feel happier and you'll find that the same concept applies to posture: physical balance contributes to emotional balance.

So keep your head up, your chin in, your chest high, pelvis and hips level, back comfortably straight and abdomen free of tension. You'll soon find that you start to feel stress-free.

For a calming yogic exercise, try the Inclined Plane. Sit on the floor with your legs straight out in front of you, toes up. Place your hands behind the line of your hips. Inhale, and rise up on your hands, keeping your feet together and the soles of your feet flat on the floor while dropping your head back as much as is comfortable. Keep your spine perfectly straight and draw your abdominal area in tightly. Contract your buttocks and thighs and keep your kneecaps facing upward. Hold. Exhale and lower your body back down to the floor.

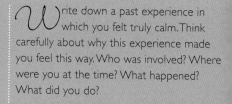

*W*rite down a past experience in which you felt truly calm. Think carefully about why this experience made you feel this way. Who was involved? Where were you at the time? What happened? What did you do?

Be as detailed about this experience as you can so that it is vivid in your mind. Think of as many descriptive words as you can to make the memory really come alive. Refer to this experience again and again to remind you that you have been calm before and that you will be again!

A mantra is a tool, a chant, word or hum that you can use to bring depth to your meditation. It works on a vibrational level in the body.

Sit in a position that feels comfortable and close your eyes. Keep your head upright, shoulders relaxed. Start to breathe steadily and deeply. Start your mantra by intoning a deep 'OH' sound from the back of your mouth and throat. Bring the sound forward in your mouth, opening it wider, as the sound seamlessly shifts into a slightly higher-pitched 'AH'. Finally close your lips and hum the sound 'MMM'. Feel it vibrate on your lips. Repeat twice more.

Take it very slowly, making the sounds as rich and vibrant as you can, and extend them for as long as you can.

Try cherry plum

The Bach Flower Remedy cherry plum is great to try if you are frightened of losing control, if you've got to the teeth-grinding, 'I'm going to murder someone' stage.

Sip a little water with a few drops of cherry plum Bach Flower Remedy in it, do some deep breathing and you will find that you regain a sense of inner calm and balance once more so that you can act rationally.

A calm sea does not produce a skilled sailor. We cannot direct the wind, but we can adjust the sails. Anyone can hold the helm when the sea is calm.

Tom Culve

News is important to us, but what you hear via the media can be highly stressful. If you hear, see or read about too much negativity, this can have a detrimental effect on you and your approach to life.

Taking one day a week to avoid seeing or hearing the news from TV, the Internet, and other sources can do you a great deal of good. If anything really important is happening, you'll hear about it from other people, but the peace and quiet will be good for reducing your stress levels.

Sometimes, the enemy is inside your head, in the form of negative self-talk. We all experience the 'monkey mind'; that seemingly uncontrollable inner voice that always seems to be telling us what to do and often being judgmental. If you suspect that you habitually use negative self-talk in your daily life, perhaps you can learn positive self-talk instead.

By keeping a journal, using positive affirmations and surrounding yourself with positive energy, you can turn things around for the better, and experience much less mental and emotional stress in life.

Do something soothing

A repetitive and creative craft activity, such as knitting, crochet or clay-modeling, can be extraordinarily therapeutic and calming. As your hands work, your mind moves into a meditational mode. It is freed up by the activity to just float.

Don't worry about being good at what you are doing. Just concentrate on the process; this is the part of the activity that is most beneficial and calming to you. Sitting still while performing repetitive movements is calming and stabilizing for many people. It can be time to collect your thoughts.

Instant calm

TAKE UP A CALMING ACTIVITY

Try:
- Knitting and crochet
- Lace-making
- Basketry and pottery
- Weaving and spinning
- Embroidery and sewing
- Patchwork and quilting
- Bread-making
- Wood-working

There is a
calmness to a life
lived in gratitude,
a quiet joy.

Ralph H Blum

If meditation is helpful to you, why not try this focused meditation technique? You focus on something intently, without needing to engage your thoughts about it. You can focus on something visual like a Buddha or something auditory like a metronome or a recording of ocean waves.

Alternatively you could try something constant like breathing or a simple concept, like 'blissful calm.' You stay in the present moment and circumvent the constant stream of commentary from your conscious mind, and allow yourself to slip into a calm state of consciousness.

Have a cup of green tea

Green tea is a natural relaxant, in part because of theanine, a main ingredient. But be careful as it also contains caffeine, though in small quantities, which might serve as an unwanted stimulant.

Focus your eyes

Look at anything, steadily, with concentration, and breathe deeply. Feel warmth in your upper abdomen; breathe and softly focus your eyes.

Perhaps you really need a holiday, and this is why you are feeling stressed, but you can't take one right now. Here's an idea: why not become a tourist without actually going anywhere? You may be surprised at how much fun it is to be one in your own town. You'll be surprised at all the nooks and crannies you've never had time to explore before.

Visit the local information center such as the public library and plan a fun time, as though you were new to your city or area. Avoid all the things that you normally do, and try out unique things that you've been meaning to do for a while, or perhaps that you'd never heard of before.

An exercise in imaginative writing will get your creative juices flowing and allow you to think about something quite outside your real life. It will give you a soothing escape hatch for a while.

Think up a scenario and then start writing about it. For example, you could imagine holding a dinner party for ten people. Invitees can be real or fictional, alive or dead. They can be from any sector of society and anywhere in the world. Who would you invite? Plan the party and the scene, just as you would a real event. Where would you hold this dinner? How would you seat your guests? What would you serve? Play the consummate host and make sure that each of your guests has someone with similar interests to talk to.

Learning to ignore things is one of the great paths to inner peace.

Robert J Sawyer

Play some games

As a child, you probably always played games. From Snakes and Ladders and Draughts to Twister, you knew how to pass the time usefully and to have fun as well. As an adult, you may think that you're too busy to play games and it's 'not for you'.

However, don't underestimate the stress-relieving benefits of a quick game of Scrabble or one of the other traditional games. They bring conviviality, companionship, competitiveness and shared enjoyment to the fore and let you relax in the moment with others.

Just about everyone spent time drawing and painting pictures when they were a child and you may well remember how focused and calm you felt. However, expressing what's inside with crayons, pencils or finger paints shouldn't just be a pastime of children and a lucky few adults who can become artists.

Whether you doodle with pens while you take a break at work, or buy some artists' supplies and go wild in your spare time, working art into your life can help you process emotions, express yourself, relieve stress, and leave you with something to frame, or at least to hang on the fridge.

> The pursuit, even of the best things, ought to be calm and tranquil.
>
> Marcus T Cicero

day 228 | Imagine the future

Do you remember how you responded when you were asked the question, 'What do you want to be when you grow up?' How do the answers you gave compare with the way you spend your time now?

If you have a lot of stress in your life, you may want to revisit the question because examining it could reveal some answers for you now. Are you really doing what you feel you were meant to do? Ask yourself what your ideal life would look like, and then take steps toward that ideal.

This yoga asana helps to relieve tension in your back and stimulates the flow of chi (the word for energy in Traditional Chinese Medicine) through your whole body.

Lie on your back, preferably on a mat or a carpet, and draw your knees up to your chest. Wrap your arms around your legs to support them. Gently and slowly rock back and forth. The pressure exerted on your spine helps to open up blockages and encourage the movement of chi.

The more you focus on problems, the more stressed out you will feel. Likewise, the more you dwell on what is working, the better you will feel. Review in your mind, or make a list of, everything that seems 'right' with your life. Think along the following lines: relationship, family responsibilities, work, friendships and home.

You may well discover that it is quite impossible to be in a stressed-out state and an appreciative state both at the same time.

For this reason, appreciation can be one of the most powerful tools for easing tension and feeling better immediately.

Take a break away from the tasks or situations that are the sources of your stress and frustration. Have a short walk or make yourself a soothing hot drink.

Of course, you will find that this does not actually get to the root cause of your problems or solve them. But it does takes you away from the source of your stress, so that you can calm down and catch your breath. It also gives you an opportunity to think about the situation more objectively.

Great events make me quiet
and calm; it is only trifles
that irritate my nerves.

Queen Victoria

Instant calm

DO A STRESS AUDIT

List all the things that press your buttons.

• Partner
• Children
• Household tasks
• Too much work
• Too little work
• Boredom
• Boss

Look within and try to pinpoint the situations that are creating the stress and negative emotions in your life. These emotions can come from a triggering event such as an overwhelming workload.

Negative emotions are also the result of your thoughts surrounding an event. For example, the way you interpret what happened can alter how you experience the event and whether or not it causes stress.

The key job of your emotions is to get you to see the problem for what it is, so you can make the necessary changes.

Experts say that pet owners have longer lives and fewer stress symptoms than non pet owners. And the sight of people happily walking dogs and generally caring for animals and relating to them is a common one.

Pets carry great stress-management benefits. Playing with your own pet (or borrowing someone else's) has a high feel-good factor. This is because it's a form of social interaction that carries no pressure to meet anyone else's expectations! So whether you're stroking a cat, tossing a frisbee to a dog, or gazing at the tranquil inhabitants of a fish tank, you can lower your stress level pretty quickly!

> Stress is an ignorant state. It believes that everything is an emergency. Nothing is that important.
> Natalie Goldberg

Let your inner child play

A fun way to reduce stress is to let your inner child come out to play. Give yourself your own toy box containing your personal art supplies and craft items, modeling clay, and a bottle of bubble solution with a bubble wand. Think five years old. Think about what you enjoyed when you were a child that you could adapt to your current lifestyle and situation.

The secret of success is to be in harmony with existence, to be always calm, to let each wave of life wash us a little farther up the shore.

Cyril Connolly

Try karate breathing

day 235

Karate breathing meditation can cause you to feel extraordinarily calm. So have a go at it today.

Sit in a comfortable position. Close your eyes; keep your back straight, shoulders relaxed and head up. Take a deep breath, expanding your belly and keeping your shoulders relaxed. Hold for a count of four. Exhale, and repeat twice. Then breathe normally, focusing attention on your breath.

As you breathe, inhale through your nose and exhale through your mouth, expanding your belly. If your thoughts drift toward the stresses of the day, gently refocus on your breathing and remain in the present. Feel the air move in and out. Continue this for as long as you like. You should notice that your body is more relaxed and your mind calmer.

245

day 236 — Comforting massage blend

Instant calm

MAKE A DATE WITH YOURSELF

When you need to calm down, make a date with yourself for an evening of quality 'you-time'.

If you find yourself with a spare evening, why not try this 'spoil-yourself' pampering regime?

First of all, indulge in something wholesome and tasty to eat. Choose something you really, really like. Then enjoy a hot bath by candlelight. Dry yourself with a warm, fluffy towel. Soothe your body with a blend of five drops of sandalwood and five drops of frankincense in 28 g (1 oz) massage carrier such as sweet almond (if you have any left over, you can store it in an amber or cobalt glass bottle). Now curl up in bed with a good read, a cup of chamomile tea and possibly your partner of choice.

Focusing on your breath is one of the best ways you can de-stress yourself quickly and effectively.

Start with abdominal breathing. Let all your breath out through your mouth and then allow your abdomen to expand as your lungs fill up again. When you exhale, say 'TEN', letting go of tension as if it is being carried out of your body with the air. Next time you breathe out, say 'NINE', and so on, all the way down to 'ONE'. When you get to 'ONE' start again. Each time you breathe out, remind yourself that you are letting go of tension.

Many people repeat this sequence slowly for a period of 15 to 20 minutes. They find that with each new countdown, they reach a deeper level of relaxation.

day **238** Unfreeze yourself

Curl up in a fetal position (on your side with your legs drawn up toward your chin), breathe deeply, and hum. You may want to rock back and forth. Concentrate on what feelings want to emerge.

day **239** Enjoy aquarium fish

Keeping an aquarium is a highly effective de-stressing therapy. Studies have shown that gazing at aquarium fish reduces stress. Even watching a tape of fish has been proven to be therapeutic.

Do you tend to act aggressively with people when simple assertiveness will work a great deal better? Or do you passively let others walk all over you because you don't know how to say 'no'?

Here are nine ways to handle conflict calmly:

- Use 'I' messages (such as 'I can understand that you might be upset, but...')
- Stay focused
- Listen carefully
- Try to see the other point of view
- Respond to criticism with empathy
- Own what's yours
- Look for compromise
- Take time-out
- Don't give up.

A day at a spa may seem a perfect way of getting some relaxation time. But if you cannot go to one or you find it too expensive, you can create your own spa-like environment at home. If you don't have body scrubs, masks or treatments you can look up recipes on the Internet and make your own.

Follow up your treatment with a hot bubble bath lit by some beautiful aromatherapy candles. And if you are so inclined, give yourself a pedicure or manicure.

The more stressed you feel before you have your DIY spa day, the more you can pamper your way into a calmer state of mind.

Working with plants and getting your hands into the soil, is incredibly therapeutic and calming. Don't worry if you don't have a garden, apartment-dwellers can still get involved. You can do your gardening in pots, instead of flowerbeds. You can have pots inside the home, by your front door and on the patio.

There is a little work involved in setting it up your pot collection and getting it established, but you'll find that tending the plants, fruits, vegetables and flowers and watching them grow, bloom, or yield is highly rewarding. You'll soon find that this kind of small-scale gardening is a great way to control stress and worry. An added benefit is the creation of a more beautiful, restful environment.

Instant calm

IS YOUR JAW HOLDING STRESS?
Wiggle your jaw from side to side to relax it.

checklist 8 How did you do?

*W*hether you tried out several ideas this month or just one, you might like to reflect on what you chose to try and why, and if it worked for you.

1. How many activities did you try this month?

- 1–3 activities ☐
- 4–10 activities ☐
- 11–20 activities ☐
- 20–30 activities ☐

2. How many did you repeat several times in the month?

- 1–3 activities ☐
- 4–10 activities ☐
- 11–20 activities ☐
- 20–30 activities ☐

3. Which activities had a positive effect on your mood this month?

Use the page opposite to make notes about what worked for you and what didn't.

Notes, jottings and thoughts

If you've had a bad shock and need to calm down, you might consider this homeopathic first aid. The remedy aconite minimizes your negative responses to physical and emotional shock and helps you on your way to recovery.

When you are feeling fearful, anxious and panicky, try 30c of aconite. It can bring you calm and comfort and help you to address the situation.

Can you remember the last time you were alone and could enjoy peace and quiet? What if you gave yourself permission to 'unplug' from the noise and distractions of this world and found time for solitude and silence?

You could help this along by taking a break from the endless noise created by radio and TV and the compelling distractions of the Internet and your phone to free up space for rest and contemplation. Why not light a few calming floating candles? Try a little solitude today and see how you feel.

Instead of activating your panic button when you get stressed, it's much more useful to activate your calm button. When something or someone agitates you and you start to spin out of control, see in your mind's eye a large button saying CALM. Create it a shape you can see easily – round and in a peaceful color. Whenever you see your calm sign, let this remind you to slow down your activities, your body and your breathing. Close your eyes and say to yourself, 'I am calm and ready to deal with this.'

Find a quiet place, and lie or sit down and close your eyes. Begin by imagining yourself outside, in your favorite place in nature. Concentrate on all the sights and sensations that you experience. Feel the warm sun on your face. Imagine the sun moving down through your body, warming and relaxing your muscles. Your body is glowing so much that it feels as though the sunlight is coming from the inside instead of from the outside.

As light rejuvenates you from the inside, the sunlight shines down and relaxes you from the outside, until you are surrounded by a large bubble of warm, bright light. As the light gets brighter you feel energy flooding into your body. All your tensions are gone, replaced by bright light filled with calmness.

When life gets a little boring and wearisome, wear something that you normally wouldn't even consider. This might be a colorful hat or an extrovert piece of jewelry. Whatever it is could be on show or hidden from view.

You don't have to go overboard, but just add that little something that's out of the ordinary. Maybe it's your Snoopy underpants that nobody has to know about, but which will make you giggle all day long.

Take control of what is within your reach and forget about, or ignore, all the things you can't control. This will make you feel more powerful and much calmer. You have the wisdom to know the difference between what you can manage and what you can't. In addition, recognize that you don't have to do everything all alone. So make the decision to ask for help whenever you need it.

If you can attain repose and calm, believe that you have seized happiness.

Julie-Jeanne-Eleonore de Lespinasse

There's a very good chance that 'no' was one of the first words you ever learnt, but it's funny how some of us quickly learn not to use it. So don't feel you have to say 'yes' to things you don't want to do, especially when you feel you're being taken advantage of! You'll only end up feeling stressed out.

Practice drawing your boundaries. Start with easy people, like a good friend, before tackling trickier customers such as your boss or your mother. And, remember, if you can't say 'no', at least don't say 'yes', say 'maybe'. 'Maybe' works because it gives you a chance to think. You can always go back and say 'no' at a later time.

Pulsatilla is an anemone and one of over two thousand species of mostly herbs and shrubs in the large *ranunculaceae* family. As a nervine it is particularly good for women. You could use the homeopathic remedy pulsatilla (30c) to calm and soothe your rattled nerves, as well as to reduce your stress levels.

There is no need to go to India or anywhere else to find peace. You will find that deep place of silence right in your room, your garden or even your bathtub.

Elisabeth Kubler-Ross

day 251 — Pawpaw for clarity

There is a calmness to a life lived in gratitude, a quiet joy.

Ralph H Blum

Making decisions is hard for many of us. It sometimes seems as though a big decision is the hardest thing of all. You may feel overwhelmed and overburdened and your stress levels may be rising beyond your control.

Pawpaw, one of the Australian Bush Flower Essences, will help you with focusing on a problem and clarity in coming to a decision.

When you are unable to solve a problem, take four drops of the essence in a little water. You'll soon feel the benefit.

Keep things in perspective

Even when facing very painful events, try to consider a stressful situation in a broader context and keep a long-term perspective on it. Avoid blowing the event out of all proportion.

Have a light lunch

Try this comforting asparagus and cheese light lunch. Toast two slices of granary bread. Place four asparagus spears on each untoasted side and grate some cheese on top. Pop under the grill until the cheese is melted.

The soles of your feet are very sensitive: full of reflex points that, when pressed or massaged, can affect the rest of your body. You could try a foot-roller to use quickly and easily at home. It will have a huge effect on your stress levels.

You operate the foot-roller by rolling your feet back and forth on it. You can do this while watching TV, reading a book or working at your desk. This massage replicates the basic push-and-release technique used by professional masseuses and reflexologists and gives your whole body a workout.

I nject a little craziness into your daily life. You may be accustomed to getting through your day without really noticing the ordinariness and seriousness of the things around you, and this may be affecting your moods negatively. Try leaving little signs and symbols around your home to remind you to lighten up. You could drape a colorful scarf over a chair, knot a bizarre tie to your doorknob, put a silly doll or small toy on top of your computer. Look around you! When you catch sight of these things in odd moments, you'll be able to raise a little smile.

265

Shiatsu for beginners

> If you can solve your problem, then what is the need of worrying? If you cannot solve it, then what is the use of worrying?
>
> Shantideva

Shiatsu is a traditional hands-on therapy originating in Japan, which corrects imbalances in the body and maintains health. Why not try it if you are feeling stressed and nervous?

Sit comfortably. Place one hand on top of the other, over your navel. Concentrate on deep breathing and hum a tune, focusing on a point two finger-widths below your navel. After a few minutes, lean forward onto your hands as you exhale. Now inhale slowly as you straighten your spine. Repeat five times. Now clasp both hands, so that they interlock in the Vs between the index finger and thumb. You are touching a major acupoint called 'meeting mountains'. Press the thumb, leaning in toward the base of the index finger. Hold the pressure for five seconds, release for five seconds. This exercise will strengthen your chi.

A creative psychiatrist had a special lampshade in his office that reflected the stars in the night sky onto his ceiling when he turned off the lights. When his patients were lying on his couch and telling him their problems, he would ask: 'How will this matter in a hundred years?'

Try to remember what was bothering you six months ago. You are unlikely to be able to remember. Somehow you have survived and resolved the situation and are now anxious about something else. Shift your down mood by putting it into a cosmic perspective. What is ruining your day today? Ask 'How will this matter in six months' time?' And notice how your mood shifts.

Have a 'me-fest'

What's good about you? Are you a nice person? Are you a good friend, daughter, mother or partner? When was the last time you acknowledged your own good qualities?

People are typically quick to complement others on their achievements, but reluctant to do the same for themselves. So have a 'me-fest' today. Or you could do this at a certain time each day. If you need to see your thoughts in print, keep an 'All About Me' journal, full of all of the great things that make you who you are.

Did you know that your head weighs about as much as a bowling ball? So if your neck gets stiff from the effort of holding it up, it's no wonder.

Periodically, throughout the day, exercise your neck muscles by turning your head slowly from side to side. Do this ten times. Next, tilt your head forward and backward ten times, gently stretching your neck muscles. Finally, lean your head slowly toward your right shoulder ten times, then toward your left shoulder.

This exercise relieves tension in your neck and shoulders, and lets chi (the term for energy in Traditional Chinese Medicine) flow more smoothly between your head and your body.

Is there someone in your life who has some habits that you don't like? Maybe you would like to change this person, but you're having little success. Is this making you feel stressed?

People are like snowflakes; each one has a different design. Do you happen to know whether anyone has ever tried to change you? How did that make you feel?

Accepting that you can't change another person and that they are doing the best they can will make you just that bit calmer.

Head-to-Knee Pose

day **261**

For a calming stretch, try this yoga pose. Sit on the floor, upright, with your arms at your sides and your legs straight in front.

Spread your left leg out to the side. Bend your right leg and place your right foot against the inside of your left thigh. Place your left hand on top of your left leg. Inhale and bring your right arm out to the right side and straight up over your head. Exhale and bend from the waist toward the left over your outstretched leg. Remain facing the front and try to bring your left ear toward your left knee. Grasp your left leg, ankle or foot with your left hand and bring your right arm over your head and parallel to your body directly over your right ear. Hold. Inhale and return to vertical with arms outstretched to sides. Exhale and lower arms to sides. Repeat on the other side.

The time to relax is when you don't have time for it.

Sidney J Harris

271

Banana melody

The feel-good chemical, serotonin, cannot be produced by the body without tryptophan, so you may need to boost your intake to improve your mood.

Why not try this delicious sunflower seed and banana melody since bananas and sunflower seeds are natural sources of tryptophan?

Cut one red apple and one green apple into small pieces and combine with one sliced banana and half a cup of sunflower seeds. Mix one tablespoon of fromage frais, half a tablespoon of honey and one tablespoon of orange juice. Combine lightly with the fruit and serve on a lettuce leaf.

Legs-up-Wall Pose

If you need to unwind at home after a hard day, you'll find this yoga pose very calming and relaxing. Do it in odd moments.

Before you get into the pose have a few blankets or rolled-up towels by your side to make yourself more comfortable.

Sit next to the wall with your knees bent and your side, shoulder and hip touching the wall. Swing around to bring your bottom right up close to the wall, supporting yourself on your elbows and forearms. Move your legs straight up the wall. After ten minutes bring your knees to your chest and gently roll out to your right side. Wait for a few minutes before you get up. Close your eyes and breathe easily and deeply to relax.

Writing an open letter to someone can be a highly cathartic experience. You could write one to anyone, from a politician to your mother, and there's no need to actually send it.

You might be feeling angry or upset with the person and penning a letter to them, which you don't send, is a positive way of externalizing your thoughts and feelings about them.

Find yourself a quiet place and write down what it is that is making you feel so strongly. Writing down your thoughts and feelings will leave you feeling calmer.

Sleep is the great healer of mind and body and it has a transforming effect. If you go to bed feeling tense and jangled, you will wake up the next day feeling fresh and calm. Sleep recharges your energy levels and all your body's systems.

Mental wellbeing is also one of the sleep-health benefits. Getting proper, regular sleep helps your mind to unwind, regroup and cope with stress. When you don't get your rest, both body and mind are less able to cope with and adjust to stressors. Sleep helps to keep the chemicals in your brain balanced and allows your mind to process out stressful or painful things from your day.

day 266

Affirm your calmness

*L*eave written affirmations on sticky notes in places where you will see them regularly. The notes can contain action affirmations, such as 'I am calm' or one of your favorite calm-inducing quotes.

It's best to use short phrases that are easy to remember and always use positive words. For example, it's better to say 'I am calm' rather than 'I am not relaxed'. When you see the affirmation, it's also helpful to say it aloud, rather than reading it to yourself.

Much of what upsets us and destroys our calm occurs because we are living too much in our heads and not enough in our bodies. So here's a simple way to get out of your head and back into your body.

Sit comfortably in Easy Pose (simple cross-legged pose) or in a chair, with both feet flat on the floor. Push both palms together and place them over your heart area in Prayer Position. Make sure the thumbs are touching your heart chakra area. Now breathe into this area by bowing your head, closing your eyes and connecting to the quiet place inside. You will notice that the longer you stay in this peaceful posture the more energy will be directed away from your head and back into your body and heart.

day 268 — *Make a thanks list*

Instant calm

JUST LISTEN
Try listening to the *Blue Danube* waltz to revitalize your nervous system and to ease your feelings of stress.

Ken Keyes was a quadriplegic who radiated love and acceptance. He wrote 'To be upset over what you don't have, is to waste what you do have.'

When you are having an off-day and want to perk up, make a list of everything in your life that you can give thanks for. Start with the simple acknowledgment that you have a roof over your head, food in the kitchen and go on to add as many things as you can. You might include having a friend and a park to sit in. Weigh the positive against the negative and notice the difference as you move from stress to calm.

If you would like to take up a calming exercise on a regular basis, water aerobics is a great choice. You could join a class or just try things out on your own. Try this exercise to tone your abs as well as to chill out generally:

Hold on to the rim of the pool with your elbows while standing with your back to the pool. Without bending your knees, slowly simulate a sitting-in-a-chair position, keeping your back in line with your limbs. Stay like this for ten seconds, breathing easily. Do this cycle four times.

Smile, breathe and go slowly.
Thich Nhat Hanh

Stay in the moment

We all make mistakes. We wouldn't be human otherwise! So don't beat yourself up and feel bad about the mistakes you made yesterday or last month.

Keep in mind that no one is perfect and that you were doing your best. Being worried about the past or fearful about the future can keep you stuck. Rather than ruminating, feeling frustrated and giving up, think 'in the now' and how you can change your way of thinking from agitation and negativity to positive pro-action and calm.

Spend time doing the things that you really enjoy. If you like going to the movies, listening to music, taking long relaxing baths, taking dance classes, or whatever, just do it!

Don't let feelings of negativity hold you back. It's up to you to make, and keep, yourself calm and happy. You owe it to yourself and to others around you. It can be difficult to find time to do something significant to honor yourself every day, but small things count, too. Read an affirmation, pick a single flower or read a chapter in a book. It doesn't have to be huge; simply enjoyable and rewarding to you.

Instant calm

HAVE A LAUGH
Laugh to invite play and joy into your life. Kids laugh 300 times a day. How about you?

Lemon balm is a member of the mint family and is an excellent herb for soothing the nerves and lifting the spirits.

To make an infusion pour a cup of boiling water onto two or three teaspoonfuls of the dried herb or between four and six fresh leaves and leave to infuse for ten minutes. Drink a cup of this tea in the morning and evening, or whenever you feel the need. Don't drink lemon balm if you have an underactive thyroid.

Instant calm

COMPUTER-BREAK
If you need to take a computer-break, close your eyes and cover them with the palms of your hands.

When you need to calm down, the technique known as 'candle-gazing' can have a wonderful effect. So give it a try!

Sit in a comfortable position with the candle on a table, at eye height, a short distance away, in your line of sight. Make sure that the room is not draughty, to prevent any flickering. Spend a few moments concentrating on your posture and your breathing. Soften your gaze and look at the flame. Concentrate on the outline and center of the flame. After a few minutes, or when your eyes feel tired, close them. You should be able to 'see' the image of the flame with your eyes closed. Keep concentrating on this image and when this starts to disappear, open your eyes and repeat the gaze. Carry on until you can hold the image without looking at the flame.

checklist 9 *How did you do?*

$\mathcal{W}$hether you tried out several ideas this month or just one, you might like to reflect on what you chose to try and why, and if it worked for you.

1. How many activities did you try this month?

- 1–3 activities ☐
- 4–10 activities ☐
- 11–20 activities ☐
- 20–31 activities ☐

2. How many did you repeat several times in the month?

- 1–3 activities ☐
- 4–10 activities ☐
- 11–20 activities ☐
- 20–31 activities ☐

3. Which activities had a positive effect on your mood this month?

Use the page opposite to make notes about what worked for you and what didn't.

Notes, jottings and thoughts

When you are ungrounded your energies are scattered and you feel tense. There isn't enough flow between your mind and your body. For example, physically you might be here reading this book, but your mind is already thinking about what you have to do tomorrow and is not fully aware of everything happening around you right now.

To become more grounded and mindful, you could try becoming aware of your breath, which helps to ground and calm you. Another idea is to walk outside in nature; this will have the same effect. In addition, making sure you are fully hydrated reduces stress on your body and grounds you, so eating and drinking regularly is vital to being grounded.

Slow down

It's amazing how we tend to fill our minds and our lives with mindless activity. Today, pay attention to your activity levels. If you are in the habit of being 'busy' all the time, think about how you could become less frenetic. Not all of your activity is mindless and meaningless, of course, but on closer examination, you may find that much of it is.

Consider what you fill your day with. How much of what you do is really necessary? How much of it nurtures you? Allowing more space in each day will enable you to slow down.

Instant calm

YOU-TIME
Create two minutes of 'priority-you' time every hour to listen to the needs of your body.

I f you're feeling overwhelmed by tasks and life in general, take the time to stop and sit down.

Close your eyes and drop your head into your cupped hands. Take in a few deep breaths and say to yourself slowly, 'Loosen up. All is well.' You might like to accompany this by considering tasks which you need to do right now, as opposed to tasks which you think you should do, but which can wait.

Argue for your limitations, and sure enough, they're yours.

Richard Bach

Creating a cake and eating it can be a highly soothing activity. So why not take the time to make one today. Try out this ultra-simple and truly delicious recipe.

Heat the oven to 180°C (356°F). Grease an 18-cm (7-in) cake tin and cut a piece of greaseproof paper to fit the base. Mix 175 g (6 oz) margarine, 175 g (6 oz) caster sugar, 175 g (6 oz) self-raising flour, 3 large eggs, 1 teaspoon baking powder, 1 teaspoon vanilla extract and a pinch of salt and stir until smooth.

Spoon the mixture into the tin and bake for 45 minutes. When the cake looks well risen and golden and the top springy, remove from the oven, let it sit in the tin for five minutes, then turn it out. When cool, split the cake horizontally, spread on some crème fraîche and add fresh strawberries.

Actively seek calmness

Actively seek calmness on a daily basis, through your actions and through your thoughts. Be aware of those times when you aren't feeling calm and use whichever techniques from this book that are possible and which appeal to you in the moment. Notice when you are calm and enjoy those times. If you are certain that you can achieve calm, the positive energy will push you forward.

The pursuit, even of the best things, ought to be calm and tranquil.

Marcus Tullius Cicero

Silence is a healing force and can help to calm you when your life has taken a hectic turn. Find a place to sit in silence. It can be anywhere that feels peaceful to you. It might be at the bottom of your garden, a secluded place in nature or in your kitchen.

Take note of all that is around you, really using all your senses to absorb your environment. Notice all the little things such as color, light, smell and touch. Treasure it, absorb it, immerse yourself in it and hang on to it for as long as possible.

Lime blossom infusion

Be like a duck. Calm on the surface, but always paddling like the dickens underneath.

Michael Caine

Infusions can be delicious, so try one made from dried lime blossom (also known as linden blossom). You may well find the effects very calming and your nervous tension much reduced.

Pour a cup of boiling water onto a teaspoonful of the blossom and infuse for ten minutes. Drink this three times per day, perhaps while you've got your feet up! If you like a little sweetness in your tea, add a teaspoonful of honey.

It's amazing how much tension you hold in your hands. So try to release the tension with the following exercise:

Clasp your hands together tightly and release. Squeeze the fingers of one hand with the other, press and release. Become aware of how your tension feels. Then nestle your left in your right hand, the thumbs gently touching each other. Remain like this and relax, breathing deeply and easily.

Instant calm

BE SPONTANEOUS
Try one of the following:
• Eat ice cream for breakfast.
• Hug the next person you see.
• Skip to your car.

293

Try this yogic breathing exercise to calm your mind and body:

Sit in a comfortable position, keeping your torso straight. Inhale slowly, keeping your mouth partially closed, contracting the back of your throat to slow down the breath. Hold for a few seconds. Exhale, again partially closing or contracting at the back of your throat to slow down the breath. This breath will make a hoarse hiss-like sound, like steam being released from a radiator. Repeat five times. As you get better at this, try to exhale for longer than you inhale.

Instant calm

THE PAUSE

Slow down and experience the pause after each one of your next three exhalations.

Try coffea cruda

Just as coffee winds up the nerves, the homeopathic remedy coffea cruda unwinds you, helping with hypersensitivity of the senses, nervous piercing headaches and sleeplessness from an overactive mind, coffee or too much excitement. Take 30c under your tongue when you are feeling wound up, to help calm the jitters.

Improve your posture

Slumped shoulders and a dropped neck stop you breathing properly and lead to tension and sluggishness. Straighten up, pull your shoulders back and down, pull your neck back, unclench your teeth, look ahead, take a deep breath and feel how good it is to stand up for yourself.

Instant calm

OVERCROWDED THINKING

When your thinking feels overcrowded, release the pressure from your head with a few gentle deep breaths and a stretch.

Rescue Remedy is a unique combination of five Bach Flower Remedies, all working on emotional imbalances associated with daily stressful situations. The Rescue Remedy combination is famous for quickly restoring inner calm and control. The little yellow bottle is the only combination remedy formulated by Dr Edward Bach over 70 years ago and is a handbag and desk-drawer essential. You can take it neat from the bottle or put it in liquid to sip.

Assuming that you get to choose your friends think carefully about the following points:

• Why not choose people who think you're great and support you?

• Stop dismissing compliments from people who think you're fabulous.

• How much time do you spend with people who make you feel good?

• Find a way to make time for the special people in your life. Don't fall into the trap of continually putting off the most important people because you're 'too busy'. Stay in touch to let them know you're thinking about them when things are difficult and time is pressured.

• Make the people you love and the people who love you a priority every single day!

Doodling distracts the logical, controlling, left side of the brain from focusing on what's stressing you, which automatically calms you down. So next time you're feeling stressed take up your colored pens and draw any big shape in one continuous line. Next, spend a few minutes filling in the outline with stars, hearts, zigzags, flowers, circles, anything you want. Breathe deeply and you'll begin to feel a deep sense of relaxation.

Act on adverse situations as soon as you can. Don't procrastinate and hope that it will go away or that you will deal with it tomorrow. Take decisive action now. By developing a sense of proactive awareness of what is happening to you now and how you are reacting, you are better able to take positive action sooner rather than later. This will help you not only to solve the problem, but will reduce your stress because the problem isn't hanging over you.

The life of inner peace, being harmonious and without stress, is the easiest type of existence.

Norman Vincent Peale

A tension headache causes a constant ache and tightness around your forehead, temples or the back of your head and neck. Try using a lavender wheat bag, heated in the microwave. The warmth around your neck will decrease muscle spasm and relax tense neck muscles. To ease an ordinary headache, place a fridge-cooled lavender wheat bag around your neck.

Tension is who you think you should be. Relaxation is who you are.

Chinese proverb

Some meditations are active; you mindfully engage in a repetitive activity, which quietens your mind and allows your brain to shift. You may not have thought so before, but ordinary activities such as gardening, eating, housework or creating artwork can be effective forms of meditation.

Before you start, take a few deep breaths, relax your body and focus your awareness on what you are doing. As you carry out the activity, focus on it totally. Engage with it slowly and purposefully on all levels.

Instant calm

REDUCE YOUR LIST

Simplify the speed of your day by reducing the number of things on your 'to-do' list. Most importantly, make sure that *you* are on your 'to-do' list. Don't forget yourself.

Mindfulness can be a form of meditation, which, like activity-oriented meditation, doesn't really seem like meditation at all. It simply involves staying in the present moment rather than thinking about the future or the past.

Stay 'in the now' by:
- Focusing on all the sensations you experience in your body.
- Focusing on where you feel the emotions are in your body.

Stress can cause hyperventilation, which is when you breathe faster and/or deeper than is necessary. Your body takes in too much oxygen and needs a balance of carbon dioxide. You don't give your body long enough to retain the carbon dioxide and it consequently cannot use the oxygen you have. This causes you to feel as though you are short of air, when actually you have too much.

So, if you find that you're hyperventilating, breathe slowly and rhythmically from your stomach. Also try and reduce the size of each breath. If you feel you cannot gain control over your breathing, breathe in and out with your hands cupped over your mouth and nose.

Anxiety may be a result of food intolerances, so it's worth investigating any possible culprits. You may notice that your anxiety symptoms are relieved by removing a certain food from your diet. (A food 'intolerance' is not the same as an actual food 'allergy', which is why an intolerance will not be detected during allergy-testing.)

If you think your anxiety is related to a food intolerance, visit a nutritionist, who will help you set up a food journal as part of an elimination process and help you to find out which foods may be increasing your anxiety.

A cup of astragalus tea

Herbal astragalus tea is particularly well known for its pleasant taste, cleansing properties, and slight calming effects, making it similar to many mild herbal supplements designed to combat fatigue and chronic stress.

You can make a tea by boiling up to 120 g (4 oz) of the fresh, whole root in 0.9 litres (2 pints) of water. A typical dose is between two and four cups per day.

Instant calm

JUST EAT!

Be kinder to your digestion. Get maximum nourishment out of your meals by never eating while walking, standing up or doing something else at the same time.

Square breathing allows you to slow down your breathing rate. Sit quietly and take in a few steadying breaths. Then inhale, counting silently 1 – 2 – 3 – 4. Hold your breath, counting silently 1 – 2 – 3 – 4. Exhale, counting 1 – 2 – 3 – 4. Hold, counting silently 1 – 2 – 3 – 4. Repeat the cycle half a dozen times. Return your breath to a normal cycle and allow yourself to remain resting quietly for ten minutes.

If you want inner peace find it in solitude, not speed, and if you would find yourself, look to the land from which you came and to which you go.

Ewart L Udall

H ave you ever suffered from low blood sugar levels? If so, this might be why you feel agitated. Everything you eat and drink is absorbed into the body and stored in the liver as blood sugar to provide you with energy. However due to stress, hormones or bad eating habits, blood sugar isn't always released appropriately. To balance out your blood sugar levels, eat breakfast, lunch and an evening meal plus a mid-morning and mid-afternoon snack. Make sure that you have a small amount of protein with each sitting, plus carbohydrates.

Yesterday is history, tomorrow is a mystery, and today is a gift; that's why they call it the present.

Eleanor Roosevelt

day 297 — Gassho Meditation

The form of meditation called 'Gassho' means 'two hands coming together'. The idea is to keep your attention focused on your breath and your middle fingers to keep you calm and centered in the present.

Sit quietly with your eyes closed; fold your hands in the prayer position with your fingers pointing up and your thumbs touching the middle of your chest. Focus your attention on the point where your middle fingers meet. Take a deep breath in and move your tongue to the roof of your mouth. As you breathe out, let your tongue fall again.

I t's easy to make the mistake of over-reacting. When it seems as though the whole world is out to get you and you feel like lashing out right away, wait! The situation at hand probably does call for a response of some kind, but don't respond straight away. And when you do respond, go slow. You'll handle a trying situation in a much calmer state, and come to a resolution sooner if you take time to assess the situation fully. Get all your ducks in a row before you decide on a response.

Instant calm

DRIVE SAFELY!

Before rushing off in your car, sit quietly for 60 seconds and take a few deep, grounding breaths to calm yourself.

Autogenic Training

Autogenic Training (AT) usually takes several weeks to learn, but it can be extremely effective if you are trying to cut down your stress levels. Try this simplified version:

Lie or sit somewhere comfortable. Take in a few deep breaths and close your eyes. Say each of the following statements to yourself six times, breathing deeply and easily throughout:

- My right arm is heavy and warm; my left arm is heavy and warm.
- My right leg is heavy; my left leg is heavy.
- My heartbeat is calm and steady; my breathing is deep and slow.
- My stomach is warm and soft.
- My forehead is cool.

Chinese licorice

Chinese licorice root stands next to ginseng in importance in Chinese herbalism and it can be very energizing and calming. It is used throughout the Orient because of its ability to build and sustain energy and this is at least partly due to its power to regulate blood sugar balance (which can cause anxiety).

Mimulus to reassure

The Bach Flower Remedy mimulus will help when you feel concrete fears, such as of dogs, spiders or being alone. A few drops in some water sipped during the day will help to calm you. Also try talking or writing about your fears to work toward practical and helpful solutions.

This breathing exercise is both calming and balancing.

Stand upright with your feet hip-width apart. Your head, hips, and ankles should be aligned, as if a string is pulling you upward from the middle of your head.

While inhaling, lift both arms as if they float upward to shoulder height. At the same time bend your knees slightly. While exhaling, lower your arms to the original position and at the same time straighten your knees. Repeat four times.

Instant calm

MAXIMIZE CALMING BREAKS
To get maximum enjoyment from your break-time hot drink, drink it away from your desk, the phone or TV.

Try out this calming blend (in your aromatherapy burner) when you need to balance your emotions. Use a mixture of 12 drops of geranium, 12 drops of lavender, six drops of grapefruit, three drops of bergamot and three drops of fennel in the burner.

Lie down on the floor with a cushion behind your head and your legs bent at right angles, resting on a chair. Breathe in deeply through your nose for a count of five and exhale completely through your mouth for a count of six. Repeat this breathing cycle ten times.

Instant calm

TURN OFF THE NOISE

Let your ears hear the peaceful sound of silence. Switch off man-made sounds (from your phone, TV and radio).

Whether you tried out several ideas this month or just one, you might like to reflect on what you chose to try and why, and if it worked for you.

1. How many activities did you try this month?

- 1–3 activities ☐
- 4–10 activities ☐
- 11–20 activities ☐
- 20–30 activities ☐

2. How many did you repeat several times in the month?

- 1–3 activities ☐
- 4–10 activities ☐
- 11–20 activities ☐
- 20–30 activities ☐

3. Which activities had a positive effect on your mood this month?

Use the page opposite to make notes about what worked for you and what didn't.

Notes, jottings and thoughts

Balance mood swings

The more man meditates upon good thoughts, the better will be his world and the world at large.

Confucius

If you're experiencing unwelcome mood swings, the Australian Bush Essence peach flowered tree could help you get back into balance again. You can also use this essence if you tend to get enthusiastic and then, for no apparent reason, suddenly lose that enthusiasm.

Are you one of those who doesn't 'follow through' on their goals? If this sounds like you, taking this essence will help you develop stability and commitment.

Turkey pita break

Have you ever wondered whether your tryptophan is low? This could be why you sometimes feel tense and stressed. The feel-good chemical, serotonin, cannot be produced by the body without tryptophan and without serotonin, you may feel low. Turkey is a natural source of tryptophan, so why not try this delicious turkey pita break?

First, heat some olive oil in a pan and fry 100 g (3½ oz) of turkey for five minutes until it is cooked through. Add half a chopped red onion and fry until softened. In a small bowl, add a little fromage frais with thyme, black pepper and parsley. Split one wholemeal pita bread and add the mixture of chopped turkey, fromage frais and fried onion to three chopped vine tomatoes, cucumber and Chinese lettuce.

He who lives in harmony with himself lives in harmony with the universe.

Marcus Aurelius

The tall tropical tree, ylang ylang, has large, tender, fragrant pink, mauve or yellow flowers. The name means 'flower of flowers' and the essential oil has a euphoric and sedative effect on the nervous system.

You could use it as a blended bath oil (with sweet almond oil or jojoba) to ease anxiety, nervous tension and stress. Why not lie back in the warm, scented water and enjoy its calming effects?

*M*ovement meditation combines breathing and gentle movements to create a calm, meditative state. It's really excellent if you need to calm yourself down.

Take several deep breaths. Then, move into a relaxed, squatting stance with your knees slightly bent and your hips and pelvis loose. Center yourself by visualizing your feet connected to the soil. Visualize the center of the Earth, from which you draw energy. Gently move your body in an undulating, snakelike, swaying motion. See yourself as a flower opening up or as an animal moving through the brush. Dance, if you like. Use sound or music to focus your attention on the movement and on the vibration. Feel the areas of your body that are tight and let the movement loosen them up.

Instant calm

FIVE MINUTES
Spend just an extra five minutes making yourself feel better with your clothes, how your hair looks, your jewelry or your make-up.

day 308 | *Reishi tea*

Instant calm

BEFORE YOU GET UP

Lie in bed for five minutes before getting up to start your day. Say hello to your body, connect with how it's feeling and ask it what it needs.

Reishi has the unique ability among medicinal mushrooms to calm and support nerve function if you are feeling stressed or anxious.

To make yourself some Reishi tea, slice the dried mushroom and simmer in boiling water for two to three hours. Strain and add a little honey or fruit juice to sweeten and drink hot or cold. You can store the tea in the fridge for up to three days. Do not use aluminum or cast iron when preparing, storing or serving Reishi tea.

Descriptive writing

By sitting still and becoming aware of what's around you, you realize how much you miss in the general hustle of the day getting from point A to point B.

Take your journal and go and sit somewhere where you can write and observe people. This might be a favorite café. Write a page or two describing what's around you. What do you see, hear, feel, smell or taste? Take a closer look at one person or object in your view and describe it in detail. Continue writing and notice how you come into the now and how calm you feel.

Breath and Navel Meditation

This Taoist meditation is a good way to develop your inner calmness.

First of all sit comfortably. Press your tongue to your palate and lower your eyelids until your eyes are almost closed. Focus on the gentle breeze of air flowing in and out of your nostrils. When inhaling, focus on your navel rising and your entire abdomen expanding like a balloon. When you exhale through your nose, follow the breath out as far as possible, drawing the inhalation down into your abdomen and making the exhalation long and smooth. You may focus attention on your nostrils or abdomen, or on both, or on one and then the other, whichever suits you best.

Roasted sunflower seeds

The feel-good chemical, serotonin, cannot be produced by the body without tryptophan and sunflower seeds are a natural source of tryptophan. Try this crunch snack when you want to give your mood a boost.

Place water and a quarter of a cup of sea salt in a saucepan. Rinse one cup of sunflower seeds and add them to the water and salt. Bring the water to a boil, then turn down to simmer for an hour. When this is done, strain the water and seeds through a colander and allow the seeds to dry on some paper towelling. Preheat the oven to 160°C (320°F) degrees. Spread the seeds on a baking tray and bake for 30 minutes, turning them frequently. Remove from the oven when the seeds have turned slightly browned and are fragrant.

Bathing with clary sage

Clary sage is native to Southern
Europe with small blue and white
flowers growing directly off the long, thin
stem. It was known in the Middle Ages as
the 'eye of Christ' and was a highly
esteemed medicine.

If you are feeling upset, clary sage will calm
your nervous system, particularly if you have
stress, insomnia and feel tense. Dilute it in
your bath to assist with PMS.

It is advisable not to use clary sage if you
are pregnant.

Create a 'calm list'

When you're feeling in a good space, sit down and create a 'calm list'. List all the things that make you feel calm, such as going for a walk, developing perspective or drinking valerian tea and pin it up somewhere where you can see it. When you're next feeling stressed, remind yourself of all the things that can help you.

I take care of myself because I learned early on that I am responsible for me.

Halle Berry

Burn incense

Fragrances can profoundly affect mental state. To reduce anxiety, stress and fear, burn incense while listening to soft music by candlelight. Use vanilla and sandalwood to soothe, lemongrass to calm tension and clarify the mind and jasmine as a warm and exotic escape from anxiety.

Never be in a hurry; do everything quietly and in a calm spirit. Do not lose your inner peace for anything whatsoever, even if your whole world seems upset.

St Francis de Sales

In mantra meditation, you pick a mantra that suits you and then repeat it mentally or out loud continuously. This technique will help develop your mental focus and sense of calm.

One of the best mantra meditations is So-Hum Mantra Meditation. In this version, as you inhale you think the sound 'Soooo', and as you exhale you think the sound 'Hummm'. 'So Hum' means 'I am That'. It implies that you and divinity are one. This mantra is great for opening the heart center and allowing unconditional love to flow.

Blue is the color of calm and is wonderful to use in your home. In fact it is so soothing that it is an excellent choice for nightwear.

Why not put some blue into your life when you want to calm down and relax? Use calming blue in a color meditation or visualization. This might mean visualizing yourself under a gorgeous, sparkling blue waterfall that cleanses and refreshes you. Or see yourself resting within a translucent egg of blue light, which offers a sense of renewal and protection.

Instant calm

GROUNDING NATURE

Ground yourself by connecting with nature. Hug a tree, sit on the grass and let your bare feet touch the Earth.

Herbal infusions are potent water-based preparations and are great for extracting the medicinal properties of dried herbs. Oatstraw strengthens the nerves and mellows the mood.

To make a calming oatstraw infusion, take 28 g (1 oz) of dried herb and place in a 9-litre (2-pint) jar. Fill to the top with boiling water, tightly lid and steep for four to ten hours. After straining, drink a cup or two and chill the rest to slow spoilage.

Any time you feel tense, try this exercise. Slowly inhale through your nose and out through pursed lips, allowing your abdomen to soften and rise on the in-breath then deflate and return to normal on the out-breath. Inhale and say silently 'Take control'. Exhale, silently saying 'I can do anything I want to.' Slowly repeat this for six to eight breaths, with the out-breath being slightly longer than the in-breath. Say to yourself as you inhale, 'I am breathing in peace.' and as you exhale, 'I am breathing out tension.' Each time you exhale, make sure you relax your face, jaw, shoulders and hands.

Mudra to calm

When you find peace within yourself, you become the kind of person who can live at peace with others.

Peace pilgrim

Mudras are hand positions that can be used to still and calm your mind. A 'mudra' is a Sanskrit word meaning 'seal' or 'sign' used by the yogis of India to describe the ritual hand gestures they practiced during deep meditation.

Try this mudra to release tension. Curl your index finger into the base of your thumb. Now bring the tips of your middle and ring fingers to the top of your thumb. The tips of your thumb, ring and index fingers are all touching. Your little finger is stretched out flat. Bring your elbows close to the side of your waist. Close your eyes and focus on soft breathing.

Use a water spray

Place a few drops, or more, of lavender, clary sage or sandalwood into a spray bottle, add water and spray. You can spray your face (with eyes closed) as oils are non-toxic, especially diluted in water. Spraying your work space after or before a meeting can ease tensions and create a more productive environment. You can add flower essences to the spray to help reduce tension and increase calm.

Marinated peanut tofu

Peanuts contain vitamin B$_3$ (niacin), which is involved in serotonin synthesis and promotes relaxation. So try this delicious, calming snack when you're feeling a little tense.

Cut 454 g (1 lb) of tofu into small rectangles. Mix together four tablespoons of peanut butter, two tablespoons of tamari and a clove of garlic with a cup of water. Place the tofu in a shallow dish and pour the liquid over it. Marinate for an hour. Remove the tofu from the marinade and place on an oiled baking tray. Bake at 190°C (374°F) for 30–45 minutes, or until crisp. Mix one-and-a-half tablespoons of arrowroot with the remaining marinade and cook over a high heat, stirring until thick. Place the baked tofu on a bed of rice. Cover with the sauce. Serve with steamed or stir-fried vegetables.

The sunshine of life is made up of very little beams that are bright all the time.

Dr John Aiken

A less crowded mind means that your nervous system can become calmer. So in your daily life, make sure that you take regular breaks from too much thinking and bring your awareness back into your body.

Do your best to have an enjoyable morning and afternoon tea away from your desk in a pleasant environment. Listen to the requests from your body for drink when you are thirsty, and stretch and move about when you have been still for a while. Never be tempted to skip a meal. There is an added bonus: a quiet mind has direct access to wisdom and insight.

Instant calm

CALMING VETIVER

Vetiver has a grounding and calming effect on your nervous system. Dab some essential oil of vetiver onto the soles of your feet just before you go to bed.

333

Squeeze a stress ball

Instant calm

HEART SMILES
Smile, then feel the
energy of your smile
flow downward into
your heart with each
inhale. Is your heart
smiling now?

Palm-sized stress balls, made from
high-density foam, soft rubber, or
polyurethane, come in a variety of sizes and
are recommended as stress-busters by
various health organizations. Squeezing
these balls can have a highly calming effect,
foster relaxation and help you regain your
energy. They work the reflexology points in
the hand when squeezed and can help if
you have repetitive strain injury (RSI).

This technique is all about letting your thoughts slide by without attaching to them. The effect can be very calming. Realize that thoughts are just that: thoughts. They don't have any power beyond what you give them. You don't have to believe them, or act on them. Just acknowledge them and let them go.

Think of your thoughts as being like cars on a fast road. They are the vehicles going by. Don't judge them or analyse them. Just watch them go past you. If you stop them, they will lose their way and get stuck on the road for longer than necessary.

Supported Downward-Facing Dog

Instant calm

RELAXING BATH
A cup of Epsom salts added to your bath water will relax your nervous system and all your muscles.

To release your mind and body from tension, try the yoga pose Downward-Facing Dog. Starting from an all-fours position on your hands and knees, take a deep inhale and, while exhaling, lift your hips and stretch them toward the ceiling. Support your head on a bolster or on two folded blankets. The right amount of head support will create a feeling of lift through your spine and quietness in your shoulders, neck and mind. To help take pressure off your wrists and shoulders, ground your heels into a folded blanket if they do not reach the floor.

Sometimes sounds can be very soothing. Rhythmic, monotonous, low-pitched, humming sounds that repeat at 60 to 70 pulses per minute are being made by items you are likely to have around your home. These may be able to help you lull your over-stimulated mind and take you to a state of calm.

Here are some items for you to try: a shower, an electric fan, a dishwasher or washing machine, a loud ticking clock, a bathroom fan turned on with the light off, a metronome set at 60 beats per minute, a radio or TV tuned to static or smooth jazz and easy-listening stations.

When you are content to be simply yourself and don't compare or compete, everybody will respect you.

Lao-Tzu

Feeling tense? Say to yourself 'STOP!' Now breathe in through your nose slowly and evenly. L-e-n-g-t-h-e-n your exhale as this helps you retain carbon dioxide, the natural tranquilizer. Pay attention to the natural pause that occurs at the end of the exhale. As the in-breath begins, direct your attention outside yourself to what is happening in the outside world. Silently pay attention to what you can see and hear.

The sigh-breath is a way of interrupting the build-up of physical stress rather than a breathing technique to do over and over again. Initially one or two sigh-breaths every half hour or so may be appropriate. Then aim to reduce the need to do it except for during particularly tense periods.

Have some hot milk

The age-old remedy of having a warm glass of milk to relax may not be such an old wive's tale after all. Milk contains tryptophan, which can help settle you down and make you sleepy.

Try this recipe. Heat a cup of milk in a cup or container in the microwave for three minutes, or until it starts foaming. Add a teaspoon of honey, a few drops of vanilla and sprinkle cinnamon (or some crumbled chocolate flake) and enjoy!

Instant calm

SAY 'AAAAAAAH!'
Take a deep breath, open your mouth, stick out your tongue. Now let it all go by saying 'aaaah!' Feel the release of toxic thoughts and tension dissolve from your jaw, neck and face muscles.

To send yourself off to calming sleep-land bliss, run a warm bath and put in a blend of 18 drops of lavender and six drops of valerian. When you come out of the bath, get yourself into a warm, comfortable bed and tell yourself a story, in fairytale style.

For example, 'Once upon a time there was a little girl/boy/etc.' or 'A long time ago in a galaxy far, far away…' and let the storyline do whatever it wants to. Remember, the idea is that you fall asleep at some point and it becomes nothing more than a dream. You can also just think about the happiest time in your life and replay it in your mind. It has the same calming effect.

Studies show that if you consume omega-3 supplements regularly, you are far better able to cope with stress. The richest sources of omega-3 are cold-water fish such as salmon, mackerel, anchovies, sardines and mackerel. Vegetarian sources consist of green, leafy vegetables such as spinach and broccoli. Flaxseeds and flaxseed oil are also good sources of omega-3, as are eggs, beef and lamb.

Instant calm

SIMPLE CHORES
Work at some simple chores. Doing some work around the house like sweeping or washing the dishes can be a great way to relieve stress, get things done and ease your mind, all at once.

When you're worried about something it is only too easy to focus on it to the exclusion of all else and get yourself worked up so that you arrive at gibber stakes.

If you feel yourself getting wound up, stop and force yourself to calm down. There are a number of practical techniques in this book. When you feel calmer, then you can look at things more rationally.

If you work on an upper floor in a multi-story building, skip the lift and climb the stairs. Make your climb work your body and mind. Climb mindfully, breathing slowly. Use the time alone to experience a connection with yourself. Pause at each landing. Catch your breath and focus for a moment on the blessings in your life.

Nothing contributes so much to tranquilize the mind as a steady purpose; a point on which the soul may fix its intellectual eye.

Mary Wollstonecraft Shelley

This mantra technique is all about forcing anxious thoughts to stop. So prepare a mantra that works for you. The 'howitzer' refers to the fact that it has to be forceful. Examples of these are: 'STOP!' or 'ENOUGH!' The moment you catch yourself with an unwanted thought or chain of thoughts, interrupt them with your forceful mental exclamation. Eventually this conditioning method will cause the anxious thoughts to die down.

Our modern lifestyle encourages us always to look for rapid results. Electronic meditation recordings can be just the answer for when you want to slow things down.

Combining relaxing sounds such as rainfall or meditative music with 'binaural beats' will encourage your brain to drop quickly into a meditative state and this will help to calm you down.

Whether you tried out several ideas this month or just one, you might like to reflect on what you chose to try and why, and if it worked for you.

1. How many activities did you try this month?

- 1–3 activities ☐
- 4–10 activities ☐
- 11–20 activities ☐
- 20–31 activities ☐

2. How many did you repeat several times in the month?

- 1–3 activities ☐
- 4–10 activities ☐
- 11–20 activities ☐
- 20–31 activities ☐

3. Which activities had a positive effect on your mood this month?

Use the page opposite to make notes about what worked for you and what didn't.

Notes, jottings and thoughts

Instant calm

CALMING HERB
Enjoy pesto for dinner!
Basil has been shown
to be a very calming
herb, so what better
way to get your fill of
basil than by making a
delicious pesto?

*L*earn to remain relaxed, even though there are stressful factors in your life. A useful technique to calm yourself down is to allow any troublesome thoughts to be present in your mind, but without fighting them. Try the following:

Be aware of the presence of worries, then deliberately switch your attention back to the awareness of your relaxed physical state. Check for any tension which has reoccurred.

Now return to thinking about the thing that is worrying you and visualize it as a picture on a page. Gradually fade or reduce that image in your mind down to a small dot.

You may need to repeat the process several times before it takes full effect.

The B-vitamins are often called the 'stress vitamins'. Although they are found in many foods, fresh meats and dairy products are the best sources for most of them. To make the most of the Bs contained in foods, avoid overcooking.

It is best to steam vegetables, rather than boiling or simmering them. If you need to add a supplement to those already available in your food, B-vitamins are generally best taken in a balanced complement such as vitamin B-complex.

Anything in life that we don't accept will simply make trouble for us until we make peace with it.

Shakti Gawain

day 337 — Watch your expectations

Do you have high expectations for yourself? Could they be too high? Are you setting yourself up for frustration and feelings of failure? Think about what leads you to getting upset. Why do things 'get' to you? Ask yourself, how important is it that things are exactly that way? Is it worth getting yourself worked up?

Choose which expectations are really important for you to hold on to and which ones are not. Holding on to too many expectations complicates your life. Simplify your life and reduce the stress!

Enjoy a chamomile bath

Both Roman and German chamomile have excellent calming properties. Roman chamomile is more effective for irritation, while German chamomile is calming to the mind (however, you should avoid using both of these oils during pregnancy).

Boil a kettleful of water and steep a handful of dried or fresh chamomile flowers. Put this water (plus the flowers) into your bath and top it up. Make a pot of chamomile tea using two teabags. Pour yourself a cup and remove the teabags. Get into the bath, soak and sip. Finally, put the teabags over your closed eyes and soak again.

Instant calm

USE OPTIMISM

No matter what you're feeling anxious about, help to make yourself feel better by taking an optimistic view. This is better than focusing on all the things that could go wrong.

day 339 | *Reduce your 'to-do' list*

If you keep a regular 'to-do' list, you may sometimes feel that it is actually adding to your stress rather than reducing it. Have a go at cutting down the number of items on it. Stick to three things and tackle those first of all; then enjoy a period of doing nothing.

You may have a sense that doing nothing at the present time is not an option. You look around and see other things that need doing. Why not think of these as distractions stopping you accepting where you are right at this moment?

So next time, before you tip into the next activity on your list, pause awhile and appreciate the space.

*N*eroli oil is also known as 'orange blossom' and is the perfect scent to give your home an air of tranquility. Neroli has a beautiful aroma, with balancing and sedative qualities; its hypnotic smell is instantly uplifting. Worn as a perfume, it helps you to maintain a calm countenance, while as a blended massage oil or diluted in the bath it helps with insomnia. If you like to blend your oils, neroli oil blends well with geranium, lavender and sandalwood.

Instant calm

CALMING MINT

Mint can help with lowering feelings of anger and nervousness, so add fresh mint to your food to feel better.

Driving meditation

If you commute to work in a car, then this one is especially for you. Turn your time behind the wheel into time for reflection. Before starting the car engine, place your hands lightly on the steering wheel and breathe deeply several times. Drive mindfully and remain aware of your mindfulness. As you drive, think about your 'to-be' list. Let words like 'compassionate', 'serenity' and 'calmness' percolate through your mind. Let grace-filled thoughts carry you in a loving manner through the day.

As the day moves on, develop the habit of paying attention to your body. Several times a day, step away from what you are doing to re-center yourself in your body. Sit down, close your eyes and take several long, slow, deep breaths while imagining the tension washing slowly out of your body. Notice your breathing getting slower and calmer. Just think about your breath and nothing else. It's OK not to be actively thinking for a while!

Zazen Meditation

The meditation technique known as 'Zazen' is based on concentrating on the breath and is a silent, seated meditation. You can sit on a chair or on the floor. Start the practice by sitting up straight and still and counting your breaths from one to ten. Count every inhalation and exhalation, starting with one. When you get to ten, start at one again.

If at any time your mind wanders and you lose count, gently bring your attention back to the breath and start again at one. As you get more proficient with this method, you can drop the counting and just start attending to the breath.

Frayed nerves

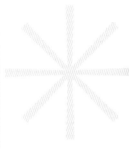

Motherwort is an effective herb. It isn't sedating, but calming, leaving you ready for action, rather than flying off the handle or bouncing off the walls. Try ten to twenty drops in a little water as soon as you feel your nerves starting to fray or just before a stressful event. Repeat every five minutes, if needed.

Ribcage breathing

To relax your mind and body, lie on your back. Contract your abdomen. Inhale slowly through your nose into your ribcage. Keep your breath focused between your ribs. Feel them expand and your chest open. As you exhale, feel the ribs contract inward. Repeat five times.

Instant calm

TAKE A NAP

One way to get your anxiety under control is to take a short nap. Sleep will relax you and let you take your mind off things.

When you're next in a stressful situation, think about what you can do and do it, one thing at a time. It's easy when you get tense to start fretting about what is out of your control or agitating about all the difficult or impossible things that should be happening. Instead, focus on what you can achieve at this moment in time and do it one step at a time. Taking this proactive and realistic stance will focus your mind and calm you down.

Cooking can be highly therapeutic and eating good food is both nutritious and calming.

For an easy nourishing stew, try this. Chop up a selection of mixed vegetables such as carrots, parsnips, onions, turnips and whatever else is available. Mix in with about 454 g (1lb) of a diced meat of your choice, pop in a couple of beef stock cubes, a chopped-up potato or two, a glassful of wine, a handful of mixed herbs and cook for around 45 minutes on a medium heat. Enjoy!

day 348

Mung bean crunch

The feel-good chemical, serotonin, cannot be produced by the body without tryptophan and mung beans are a natural source of tryptophan. Try out this easy recipe:

Soak 250 g (9 oz) of mung beans overnight. Drain and dry thoroughly. Fry in vegetable oil over a moderate heat, turning frequently, until they are browned and crisp. This will take between five and ten minutes. Now drain them on kitchen paper, sprinkle with sea salt, and cool. They store very successfully in airtight jars.

Step back and examine the world in which you live. Appreciate that you are a spiritual being who happens to be in this place at this time.

Look up into the night sky and look at the stars. Think about the vastness of the known universe. Then think about the vastness of the unknown universe. If you think you have a problem, how big does it seem now? In the grand scheme of things, whatever problem you have, it's really not that big. When you frame your problem in this way, it becomes small, even solvable.

Lie down and take several deep breaths, expanding your belly and chest with each inhalation. As you exhale, say to yourself 'breathing out' and as you breathe in say to yourself 'breathing in'.

When your mind spins off to think about tonight's dinner, simply label it 'thinking' and return your attention to your breath. When you become aware of your breath and learn to observe your thoughts, your buttons won't be pushed as easily. You'll be able to temper your reactions to difficult situations.

God, grant me the serenity to accept the things I cannot change, the courage to change the things I can, and the wisdom to know the difference.

Dr Reinhold Niebuhr

Becoming aware of your thoughts for a few minutes, a few times a day, can be calming and energizing. Stop and ask yourself 'How have I been talking to myself over the last hour or two?', 'Have I been using a negative tone or have I been talking in an encouraging way?', 'What mental images have I been dwelling on?'

As you do this, remain aware that it's not the new start that you are going to make tomorrow, or next week, that is going to make you calm; it's how you are managing your thinking from one hour to the next.

Tryptophan snack

SHIFT ATTENTION
Fight your anxiety by temporarily shifting your attention to something unrelated to what you're upset about. You may find that afterward you feel much better about the situation and are far more relaxed.

Spinach and sunflower seeds are natural sources of tryptophan. This is all-important for the manufacture of the feel-good chemical serotonin, without which you may feel low. Try this delicious tryptophan-containing snack.

Wash about 680 g (1½ lb) of fresh spinach. Cook it in a little oil until it wilts. Add one tablespoon of the sunflower seeds and a pinch of garlic and cook for two minutes. Season with black pepper and serve.

Feeling stressed? Take off your shoes and go barefoot. Take a walk on the grass and really concentrate on feeling the ground beneath your bare feet. If you don't have any grass nearby, walking on warm carpet or cool flooring can be just as grounding and calming. Draw your awareness down to your feet and the sensation of going barefoot. Get out of your head and into your body and feet.

Find a comfortable place to sit quietly and relax. Allow your breathing to become slower and more shallow. Initially this may be difficult to do for more than a few seconds. What you are doing is developing a gradual ability to tolerate slight 'breath hunger'. If you find yourself gasping or gulping or beginning to breathe even a little more deeply during your practice then you are overdoing it.

With some practice you will be able to make your breathing more shallow whenever you find yourself becoming stressed. Why does it work? Mainly because you are building up your reserves of carbon dioxide, which is your natural tranquilizer.

*N*amed for the patron saint of spiritual retreats and exercises, ignatia, a small tree, gives us the emotionally and physically supportive St Ignatius bean. In homeopathic form, this remedy treats a wide range of symptoms that can be caused by emotional stress.

Nervous debility caused by loss, living in stressful situations, frustration and disappointment or long, intense periods of study can all be soothed by ignatia (30c).

Instant calm

SLOW DOWN

If you're feeling stressed, give yourself a break and just slow down. Getting yourself worked up to rush around won't help, so take a break and let yourself relax.

HAVE HEALTHY SNACKS

Some studies have suggested that low blood sugar can be a major contributor to anxiety. Make sure your body is running on a full tank by having a healthy snack.

In this relaxed position you will find it easy to become attentive to the flow of the breath through your body, especially in your abdomen and chest. This can have extraordinarily calming effects.

Lie down with your spine supported on a bolster and your head supported slightly higher on a folded blanket. Bending your knees out to the sides, cross your ankles and let your legs relax. Support your thighs and knees with blankets to release any tension in your legs. Your arms should rest by your sides. After a few minutes, change the cross of your ankles. To open your chest further, hold your elbows and reach your arms over your head.

For a feel-good factor both on your face and in your tummy, try this edible chocolate facial. You will find that cacao beans (available as 'cocoa powder') are stress-busters due to the high levels of magnesium they contain.

Mix together three tablespoons of dark honey, four tablespoons of raw cacao (cocoa powder) with two to four tablespoons of crème fraîche and a little oatmeal to bind, to create a slightly thick, smooth paste. Put some on your face, eat a little and then lie back to relax.

When you experience situations that make you feel anxious or powerless your thoughts may turn to memories from your childhood when you experienced spells of fear or loneliness. When children feel small and helpless they look to their parents or guardians for the protection they need.

Take a moment to be a caring and loving parent to your inner child. Let her (or him) know that you will get the two of you through this stressful period. Give yourself a mental hug.

Hugging is organic, naturally sweet and contains no artificial ingredients. It is therapeutic, healing and calming. You cannot give one without receiving one in return. According to family therapist Virginia Satir, you need four hugs a day just for survival, eight hugs a day for maintenance and 12 hugs a day for growth. What's your daily hug quota?

Foot massage

Instant calm

TAKE EXERCISE
Few things can help relax you more quickly than a little bit of vigorous exercise.

Reflexology, the foot massage technique that works on the whole body, tells us that certain parts of the feet relate to certain organs and energy channels in the body.

Gently massaging both your feet (soles, ankles and toes) with warmed almond oil for five to ten minutes can soften and relax many parts of your body. Adding a few drops of an essential oil such as vetiver, sandalwood or lavender will add a calming boost to the massage.

Buy an aromatherapy roll-on. This is a small bottle the size of a lip-gloss stick with a roll-on top like a deodorant. A quick roll on your temples, wrists or neck can offer you instant therapeutic support, depending on the essential oils you use.

Try lavender essential oil to relax you, vetiver essential oil to ground you or rose essential oil to calm you down.

Happiness is as a butterfly, which, when pursued, is always beyond our grasp, but which, if you will sit down quietly, may alight upon you.

Nathaniel Hawthorne

Do absolutely nothing for five whole minutes. Withdraw your energy, attention and senses away from the outside world. Being still allows you to regroup your scattered energies back into yourself. Being still triggers a whole lot of different responses in your body. Stillness is calming.

After you've driven somewhere, try sitting in your car for five minutes before you get out, or arrive early at an appointment so that you can sit and be still. Stillness is not slouching on the couch watching TV, it's simply you spending time with just you.

Water is a powerful spiritual symbol. As you shower, visualize the water helping to cleanse out your stress.

- Feel and imagine the water swirling around your feet clockwise, then counterclockwise.
- Feel the water permeating your body into the core of your being.
- Imagine the water binding with all your stress as it climbs upward, to burst out of the top of your head like a fountain.
- Feel the water falling and rolling down your body, binding any residual stress that may be there as well.

Continue this until you feel completely cleansed. Ask Mother Earth to recycle this water as it swirls away. Feel and know that you are now cleansed and calm on every possible level.

This Sanskrit phrase means 'The jewel in the heart of the lotus.' and is excellent for lifting the spirits and calming the mind. Find a comfortable place to sit, close your eyes and take a couple of slow, deep breaths. Repeat 'Om mane padme hum' out loud or silently for ten minutes. If your mind wanders, gently bring it back to the sound of 'Om mane padme hum'.

If there is light in the soul, there will be beauty in the person. If there is beauty in the person, there will be harmony in the house. If there is harmony in the house, there will be order in the nation. If there is order in the nation, there will be peace in the world.

Chinese proverb

Smile. Release any worry, stress and tension by relaxing your facial muscles. Picture softening your forehead, cheeks, eyes, tongue, ears and scalp. Keep your mouth slightly open. This unlocks the tension in your jaw and neck. Let your tongue float in your mouth. Use a mirror to check in with your face muscles.

> If we have no peace, it is
> because we have forgotten that
> we belong to each other.
>
> Mother Teresa

*W*hether you tried out several ideas this month or just one, you might like to reflect on what you chose to try and why, and if it worked for you.

1. How many activities did you try this month?

* 1–3 activities ☐
* 4–10 activities ☐
* 11–20 activities ☐
* 20–31 activities ☐

2. How many did you repeat several times in the month?

* 1–3 activities ☐
* 4–10 activities ☐
* 11–20 activities ☐
* 20–31 activities ☐

3. Which activities had a positive effect on your mood this month?

Use the page opposite to make notes about what worked for you and what didn't.

Notes, jottings and thoughts

Conclusion

Having worked through this book, you now have a wider understanding of how stress can affect you. You also have experience of using different activities to help calm you down. Some activities have probably worked well, while others may not have had much of an impact.

Now is the time for reflection, to think of how the book has affected you. How have you changed as a result of some of the activities? What might you change in your lifestyle as a result of what you have read? Which activities could you incorporate into your daily life which are achievable and practical? By increasing activities that are calming, you will reduce your stress levels. This in turn will improve your mental and physical wellbeing.

Remember, you are not looking to eradicate stress from your life. That is unrealistic. What you are aiming for is to manage and reduce stress through daily activities that help keep you calm. So every day, use one idea to influence how calm you feel.

380

Notes, jottings and thoughts

Notes, jottings and thoughts

Notes, jottings and thoughts

Notes, jottings and thoughts